ACE Personal Trainer Study Manual

ACE Personal Training Prep Book and Practice Test Questions

Free *From Stress to Success* DVD from Trivium Test Prep

Dear Customer,

Thank you for purchasing from Trivium Test Prep! Whether you're looking to join the military, get into college, or advance your career, we're honored to be a part of your journey.

To show our appreciation (and to help you relieve a little of that test-prep stress), we're offering a **FREE** *From Stress to Success* **DVD by Trivium Test Prep**. Our DVD includes 35 test preparation strategies that will help keep you calm and collected before and during your big exam. All we ask is that you email us your feedback and describe your experience with our product. Amazing, awful, or just so-so: we want to hear what you have to say!

To receive your **FREE** *From Stress to Success* **DVD**, please email us at 5star@triviumtestprep.com. Include
"Free 5 Star" in the subject line and the following information in your email:

1.   The title of the product you purchased.

2.   Your rating from 1 – 5 (with 5 being the best).

3.   Your feedback about the product, including how our materials helped you meet your goals and ways in which we can improve our products.

4.   Your full name and shipping address so we can send your FREE *From Stress to Success* DVD.

If you have any questions or concerns please feel free to contact me directly.

Thank you, and good luck with your studies!

Alyssa Wagoner
Quality Control
alyssa.wagoner@triviumtestprep.com

Contents

Introduction

Interested in joining the fitness industry? Not a bad idea—despite, or perhaps because of, national concerns over obesity, Americans are now more willing than ever to hand over money to be active rather than sedentary. According to the International Health, Racquet & Sports Club Association, health enthusiasts spend more than 21.4 *billion* dollars on gym memberships. That's more than consumers spend on video games, and over twice as much as they spend on movie tickets.

That's obviously good news for those looking to pursue a career in the health and fitness industry. And if you have your sights set on that field, chances are you've investigated the possibility of becoming a personal trainer: an expert in cardiovascular and muscular improvement who is able to provide clear and concise one-on-one instruction to achieve an individual's goal of better health.

And make no mistake: such skills can be lucrative. Salaries vary, but recent estimates report that qualified personal trainers can earn an average of $53,323 a year—given proper experience, credentials, and education.

But just as you'd never hire an unlicensed plumber, few will seek the guidance of a trainer without credentials. That's where the American Council on Exercise (ACE) comes in. Developed as a sanctioning body for fitness instruction, ACE provides a comprehensive testing program that measures an individual's capacity to supervise an exercise regimen. By passing its exam, personal trainers will be able to offer services as ACE-approved practitioner. Both health clubs and clients will trust that a recognized name in fitness has audited their employee's ability to provide safe and proper instruction.

While other exams from various organizations are available, ACE is rare in that it offers trainers opportunities to expand their knowledge base into areas like group training or specialized health coaching. Those who are affiliated with ACE have also expressed appreciation for the Council's deep well of information resources, including the latest research, workshops, and online courses.

Now that you understand why the ACE "seal of approval" is an important step in becoming a personal trainer, you may wonder how it evaluates applicants. The ACE Personal Trainer Certification Exam is an intensive 150-question multiple choice test that demands the right preparation, knowledge, and commitment.

Sound overwhelming? Don't worry: by purchasing this study guide, you've demonstrated an understanding of what it takes to be ready on exam day. With the right attitude and information, you stand an excellent chance of becoming one of ACE's certified personal trainers.

Let's take a closer look at what the ACE exam is and what you can expect.

Getting to Know the ACE Personal Trainer Certification Exam

Before getting into the specifics of the test itself, you should have an understanding of what's expected from applicants before they put pencil to paper (or mouse to computer).

ACE exams are performed on a regular basis at more than 500 locations across the United States using both computer-based testing (CBT) and pencil and paper (PAP) exams. If you prefer the CBT option, your test results will be given to you immediately; pencil and paper results are available via mail or online four to six weeks following the exam. The test typically takes three hours, with applicants asked to arrive one hour prior to the start time in order to present proper documentation and receive instructions.

To pre-register for either test, log on to www.acefitness.org no later than thirty days prior to your preferred test date. (For CBT testing, you may register up to ten days prior.) To receive an admissions ticket that will grant you entry to the test site, you will need to meet the following criteria:

- Be at least eighteen years of age with photo ID (driver's license, military ID, passport).

- Provide proof of cardiopulmonary resuscitation (CPR) and automated external defibrillator (AED) course education at the time of registration. ACE will not accept any endorsements from online courses. (If you opt for the pencil and paper test, you do NOT need proof of CPR and AED at the time of registration, but MUST provide both before test results are released to you.)

- Pay an exam fee of $399, applicable to either CBT or PAP options. ACE accepts check, credit card, or money order. You will have until midnight the night before the test date to reschedule; doing so will incur a $149 rescheduling fee for CBT, or $169 for PAP. If you wish to cancel the test outright, provide a written request no later than thirty days prior to the exam date in order to receive a fifty percent refund of your fee.

Why opt for pencil and paper over CBT, or vice versa? If you do not yet have CPR or AED certification, opt for the written exam; otherwise, CBT offers both more flexible dates and immediate test results.

Breaking Down the ACE Personal Trainer Certification Exam

The ACE Personal Trainer Certification Exam places high demand on candidates to study and understand both basic and advanced principles of exercise and fitness, human anatomy, program adjustment for variables (pregnancy, preexisting conditions, etc.), risk factors, nutrition, client interaction, and customized program design.

While this may sound overwhelming at first, you'll quickly see that breaking down this scope of information into digestible sub-sections will make it easier to focus and grasp principles before moving on to the next subject.

The ACE test is divided into fifteen *tasks* spread across four *domains*. Each domain requires the examinee to utilize his or her knowledge of the following:

Domain I: Client Interviews and Assessments (31% of the test)
In this domain, applicants will be tested on their knowledge of how to best communicate with clients to discover their special needs and design the best program to facilitate their goal. Knowing how to observe clients to evaluate their current abilities requires an understanding of kinesiology and cardiovascular/muscular assessment.

Domain II: Program Design and Implementation (33% of the test)
Here, applicants must demonstrate their understanding of how best to apply the knowledge gleaned from their client profile to design and/or modify a fitness program suited to the client's needs. Muscular and cardiovascular adaptations, laws of motion, and understanding of safe technique will be covered.

Domain III: Program Progression and Modifications (19% of the test)
Once the client is involved in a fitness program, it will be up to the personal trainer to oversee his or her adherence to it. Topics covered in this domain include how to deal with social or physical interruptions in motivation, educating the client on proper nutritional habits, correcting lapses, and recognizing underlying causes for apathy (low self-esteem, eating disorders, etc.).

Domain IV: Professional Safety, Conduct, Risk Management (17% of the test)
Because personal training can result in the potential for liability, applicants will be required to demonstrate an understanding of basic "scope of practice" issues. Topics include: CPR, emergency protocol, inspecting equipment for proper safety, liability insurance, filling out accident reports, record-keeping, recognizing good sources to keep abreast of fitness advances, and factoring weather and temperature changes into exercise regimens.

Together, these four domains make up the 150 questions on the exam. *However, only 125 questions will count toward your test score.* ACE frequently rotates twenty-five "test" questions into the exams to gauge their applicability in the test. Because applicants never know which questions "count" and which questions don't, you'll have to be on your toes for all 150.

A perfect score is 800—but don't worry, as that's rarely achieved. To pass and receive ACE accreditation, you only need a score of 500.

Let's Make a Plan

Before we get into the specifics of the ACE exam—and fitness knowledge in general—it's important to lay down some ground rules to help you get the most out of this study guide. Everyone is different, and if you feel you absorb information best with a barking dog and blaring rock music in the background, don't let us stop you! But for the majority, keeping the following guidelines in mind will help you be as prepared as possible on exam day.

Give Yourself Time
The scope of the ACE exam asks a lot of those who take it: knowledge of everything from nutrition, to anatomy, to legal issues. It's a substantial amount of information to digest, and it can't be done in a weekend. Give yourself a *minimum* of one month of study before taking the test (ideally two): for example, a week for every chapter.

Take a Break in the Middle of Something Interesting
It can be hard to resume study after going for a stretch, a bite to eat, or a good night's sleep, but if you're pursuing personal trainer accreditation, it's likely you already have an interest in the topics covered. When you come across something that stands out as particularly intriguing, try stopping your lesson: you'll be more eager to get back to work after a break.

Get Active
Need help remembering the names of muscles? Stand up and do some stretching, flexing or pointing to each muscle as you learn its name, function, and other details. At the grocery store? Look at labels to see if you understand macronutrient breakdowns and ratios. You have some built-in study aids: your own body, as well as your daily activities. Use them!

Grab a Partner
At the end of a week's study, get a friend or family member to grab this guide and quiz you on material you've covered in the preceding week. This will prepare your mind to recall specific bits of information on demand.

On Test Day
Applicants for the ACE Personal Trainer Certification Exam are expected to arrive one hour prior to their scheduled start date. You will NOT be allowed to bring purses, cell phones, electronic devices, or any food or drink, so make sure you've fueled up prior to entering the room.

Have your admissions ticket—received when you registered—ready, as well as photo ID and your CPR and AED certificates if you're taking the computer-based test. Bring a sweater in the event the room is cooler than you'd like.

Remember that, as is often the case with multiple-choice tests, there could be two or more good answer choices. It will be your job to determine which is the *most correct* or *best* answer based on ACE's criteria.

After the Exam
As stated earlier, applicants taking the ACE exam using a computer will be able to receive their results immediately, along with temporary proof of certification: a more formal letter of accreditation and card will arrive in the mail in the following weeks. If you have taken the test using pencil and paper, results will be available via www.acefitness.org or by mail in four to six weeks.

If you have failed to successfully complete the exam, don't despair: ACE allows you to retake it as many times as you like. The fee to repeat the exam within one year is $199. After one year, applicants will have to remit the entire $399 fee. (Study this guide carefully and you may save yourself both time and money by getting it right the first time.)

Finding Employment
Accredited ACE trainers are free to pursue career opportunities. ACE does not offer job placement, though members can take advantage of marketing and business resources via their account at www.acefitness.org.

Referrals, job applications, or self-employment are typical avenues for those looking to pursue careers in personal training. Let's take a look at the pros and cons of each:

Working with a Health Club
Why share joint custody of clients with a health club? Easy: all of your customers are already in one place and ready to begin building a professional relationship with you. You'll also appreciate a more structured schedule: instead of clients demanding your attention at odd hours, you'll both be working around business hours. But be aware that clubs often seek personal trainers with experience under their belt: an eager face and an ACE accreditation may not be enough to land a job with them at the outset. You'll also be splitting commissions with the gym by as much as fifty percent.

Becoming Self-Employed

If you'd rather not work with a health club to build a client base, then you've effectively joined the ranks of the self-employed. Working as a personal trainer independent of a business demands understanding of liability insurance (you need it), proper scope of practice, emergency procedures, and the ability to create safe workout environments whether your client comes to you or you go to them.

While most of these topics are covered on the ACE exam, you'll also want to consult with a tax attorney about your responsibilities when filing as a small business entity, as well as possible deductions for equipment or use of property space.

Promote Yourself

Whether you align with a gym or turn your garage into your office, getting your name and brand out is of paramount importance. Cast your net wide to increase your chances of building and maintaining a dedicated group of customers. Maintain a Facebook and Twitter presence. Leaving business cards at amenable locations is a low-tech but an effective way of drumming up income; talking-up potential clients in social situations is also recommended.

It is important for you to remember that ACE has a national reputation for holding the highest standards in fitness and education. As a fitness professional with ACE certification, you will receive career-long support from ACE through additional training, education, and certification.

So now that you have your information and your plan, let's get to studying!

Domain I: Client Interviews and Assessments

THE INTERVIEW

You've heard it before, and we'll say it again: First impressions are crucial to the success of a relationship. During the initial meeting with your client, there are various factors that you need to take into consideration. Remember these concepts! Once established in the initial meeting, they will need to be maintained throughout the entirety of the working relationship.

Rapport, Trust, and Credibility

Even if "first contact" with your client takes place over the phone, it is absolutely essential for fitness professionals to immediately establish **rapport**—a strong connection based on trust and a sense of camaraderie. Why is this important? A client who feels comfortable and well-understood has many advantages to success, including possessing more motivation, a greater ease in sharing personal goals and facing obstacles, and an increased willingness to follow instructions, among others.

That's all well and good, but how does one go about establishing rapport? You can't simply walk up to a stranger and say, "It's important that you trust and feel comfortable with me," while expecting immediate results. (If only it were that easy!) While that phrase may in fact be helpful, the best approach to use during the initial meeting involves **listening to** and **observing** new clients **without judgment** or **criticism**. At this stage of the relationship, trainers must display a supportive attitude and demonstrate sincere **empathy**—the ability to relate to a person's state of being. Empathy is more powerful in relationship-building than sympathy, which is simply acknowledging a person's state of being and offering comfort: empathy creates a stronger interpersonal connection.

This could be difficult, especially if the client is in a situation which you've never before experienced; but empathy is all about creating personal connections.

Say a client comes in for an initial meeting. He has been struggling with obesity his entire life, and he is extremely frustrated that he hasn't been able to successfully meet his weight loss goals. You yourself have never exceeded an average BMI, and so cannot relate directly to his situation.

How will you establish empathy, then?

Perhaps you've never experienced the emotional pain of being overweight for years, but a good health professional will recognize the state of being such a circumstance can invoke (for example: embarrassment, shame, etc.). Although you've never been overweight, everyone understands pain and frustration, and what it's like to have seemingly unattainable goals. Try to create an empathetic link that way.

> *Important Note*: In situations such as these, where you do not have a direct empathetic experience, take care not to use phrases such as, "I know exactly how you feel." Such phrases can be frustrating to clients, especially when they personally identify with their struggles. Instead, be specific. Statements like "I know what it's like to have goals that seem impossible" or, "I myself suffered for years from a speech impediment, so I know what it's like to feel as if you don't fit in" show the client that you understand his or her situation. Identifying with a client's personal situation is essential to establishing rapport.

By building rapport, you also lay out the foundation for **trust**. Without trust, clients will not reach the level of comfort necessary to openly discuss their needs and fears with you. A foundational level of trust develops when personal trainers are authentic and enthusiastic about helping clients succeed.

Along with trust comes **credibility**: whether or not your client can trust you as a *professional*. Leadership qualities like punctuality, professional conduct and appearance; showing dedication; and working as a positive role model are effective traits in establishing credibility. However, the most important ways to establish credibility are by demonstrating a solid knowledge of your field, by having up-to-date certification, and by demonstrating familiarity with current issues.

As important as it is to appear knowledgeable, you must also respect the limits of expertise. Never fake it. In fact, credibility actually improves when you first admit that you are not authorized to respond or advise on certain matters, and then offer to find the necessary information. A referral to a qualified professional such as a massage therapist, dietician, physical therapist, paramedic, etc. may also be necessary in these cases.

Never prescribe any type of exercise, therapy, or diet beyond your qualifications. To know when a referral is necessary, get to know your clients. Their medical history and current level of fitness will allow you to determine the severity of such conditions as fatigue, muscle soreness, or joint pain.

Laws for medical clearance and referrals vary from state to state, so be familiar with the rules that govern your particular region.

Comfort
It's hard for a person to be comfortable emotionally when they can't be comfortable physically. Make sure that your initial meeting (and indeed, all future meetings) takes place in a relaxing and calm environment that is free of distractions. Ask your clients if they are comfortable with the room's temperature. Use moderate lighting. Invest in some comfortable chairs! If the initial meeting occurs over the phone, ask if this is the best time for the client to speak with you and offer to call back when it is more convenient.

During the Interview

Many professionals utilize **questionnaires** immediately before a client interview. These questionnaires can include such questions as:

1. What are your main goals? What would you like to get out of this experience?

2. Please explain your level of experience in physical activity.

3. Do you have any health issues that I should be aware of?

4. Any other questions you may have as a result of the conversation.

The PAR-Q form, which we'll discuss in a later part of this chapter, is one such questionnaire that can provide a wealth of background information. However, it is imperative that you gather information in an interview setting to get a full picture of a client's needs.

Components of an Effective Interview

Interpersonal communication skills are essential for building and maintaining rapport and trust. Work to become an **active** and **attentive listener**, letting the client know through verbal and non-verbal gestures that you are engaged in the conversation. Nodding the head, using expressions that correlate with what is being said, paraphrasing where appropriate, and using eye contact all convey active listening.

- Show involvement and interest with an open, relaxed posture.

- Maintain an easy gaze at the triangle between the eyes and mouth.

- Never look around the room or at your watch when a client is speaking.

Non-Verbal Communication

Effective communication involves paying attention to emotions, body language, and non-verbal cues. Be fully present during the entire meeting by using open body language. The following are major examples of *closed* body language—avoid them!

1. **Crossing Your Arms, Legs, Feet, etc.**: People cross their limbs when they are closing themselves off or distancing themselves from a situation. An uncomfortable person may cross their arms over their chest, as if protecting or shielding themselves.

2. **Raised or Lowered Chin**: A raised chin connotes superiority or disinterest. A lowered chin suggests vulnerability or aggression. Keep a level, relaxed gaze instead! Keeping the head cocked to the side also implies attentive listening.

3. **Clenched Fists**: It may come as no surprised that clenched – even closed! – fists symbolize anger or aggression. On the other side of the spectrum, relaxed, crossed hands suggest engaged listening; open, upwards-facing palms encourage emotional connections.

4. **Indirect posture**: Any posture which obscures a straight-on view of the body functions the same as crossed limbs, sending a "keep away" message. Face your client directly.

Don't just watch your own body language though: keeping the above examples in mind can help you determine the emotional state of your client as well. If you notice any of these, don't address them directly by saying, "I can tell by your crossed arms that you're upset." Instead, ask the client how she is feeling, or if there's anything that she'd like to address. If she refuses, then respect her desire for privacy while reiterating that you wish for her to be completely comfortable.

Verbal Communication

As mentioned above, verbal responses demonstrate active listening. Even when you don't fully understand what a client is explaining, provide feedback. Use **clarifying statements** such as, "Can you help me better understand what you meant by…" or, "Could you tell me again about…?" This tool allows the client to feel reassured while avoiding miscommunication.

Be sure to ask clients questions that require more than a simple, one-word answer. Asking **open-ended questions** provides a chance to gain valuable insight:

1. What types of activities did you do when you were a child/school-aged?

2. How have your eating habits changed over the past several months or years?

3. How do you think your life would improve if you reached a higher level of health and fitness?

4. What specific areas would help you the most?

Probing is another verbal form of active listening which helps further information about a subject that has been previously discussed. This is accomplished through **continuing phrases** such as "Can you tell me more about…?"

Throughout the interview, pay particular attention to subjects about which the client seems passionate. Whenever he or she becomes uncomfortable or seems to close off, bring the conversation back to the topic that interested him or her with a probing statement. For example, if a client lights up when discussing a son or daughter, but closes off after approached about his or her dietary habits, then ask a question concerning the child's activities to engage the client once more.

Important Note: Keep your opinions to yourself unless asked!

HUMAN BEHAVIOR

Understanding a person's ability to make permanent lifestyle changes is crucial to health fitness professionals. Your client's attitudes, perspectives, and motivations will influence all of your interactions. You cannot simply regurgitate information to your client and expect a response. There is much more involved: keeping your clients happy and satisfied; knowing the proper way to instruct your audience; and, above all, making permanent, positive health changes in peoples' lives.

Learning Theories

The four standard learning theories are: behaviorism; cognitivism; constructionism; and humanism.

Behaviorism simply views learners as observers who develop, or learn, their behavior based on the type of outside feedback they receive. When people receive positive feedback following an event or action, they learn to repeat the behavior that caused that event or action to occur, while negative feedback prevents reoccurrences.

> For example: Touching a hot stove leads to pain—negative feedback—and so a person learns not to touch the stove again.

The learner is viewed as passive until acted upon by environmental stimuli (this behavior is also called **operant conditioning**). One way to understand behaviorism is to remember that people learn through feedback from their *actions*, or how they *behave*.

Cognitivism replaced behaviorism in the 1960s as the dominant paradigm of learning. Instead of understanding learned behaviors as responses to stimuli, cognitivism argues that a person's learning process is affected by his or her own unique thinking, memory, and problem-solving abilities. Think of the mind as a computer: information comes in and is processed, leading to certain outcomes.

14

Constructionism builds on the idea that people have unique sequences of learning experiences and further holds that these past experiences affect the way people process new information. Under this theory, learning becomes an active, *constructive* process, where people link new information to prior knowledge in order to build upon their own subjective representations of objective reality.

Humanism, the final and most complex theory, holds that learners must be evaluated entirely in order to understand, interpret, and predict their reactions to new information. Each person's learning is unique and personal to his or her own self. Combining both affective and cognitive values, this theory emphasizes the potential in every *human*. Humanist learning is student-centered and personal, seeking to ultimately develop confident and self-actualized people in a supportive setting.

After becoming familiar with these learning theories, remember that every person's ability to learn is affected by the type of feedback he or she receives, in addition to social background, life experiences, current beliefs and internal disposition. To help clients learn to be fit, professionals must design unique and specific programs accordingly.

Learning Phases

In addition to understanding the four standard learning theories, health fitness professionals can further help clients achieve fitness goals by providing appropriate input during each of three learning phases. These phases occur in the following order:

1. **Cognitive**: Clients focus on learning the basics of a particular exercise or weight machine. Because the activity is new, they must first think about every move before executing it. Full attention will be given to the instructions and guidance; therefore, health fitness professionals must deliver thorough instructions in order to build the client's confidence levels.

2. **Associative**: This is where muscle memory comes into play. At this point, clients become more comfortable with an exercise and can rely on muscle memory to perform the basic mechanics. They will still depend upon corrections on form or technique, so be prepared to provide constructive criticism at this stage.

3. **Automatic**: Finally, in this phase of learning, clients can perform an exercise efficiently without giving much thought to proper form or technique. Muscle memory will help them automatically make corrections. Positive feedback and further instruction (if necessary) are appropriate in this phase.

What Affects Behavior?

These next theories focus on variables that affect human behavior and explain why people can lack motivation to improve their lives.

The **Health Belief Model** is one such theory that can help identify psychological reasons for a person's inactivity by evaluating their current attitudes and beliefs as a set of variables, depending upon individual perceptions, modifying factors, and the likelihood of action. Note the chart on the following page for how these factors are all related.

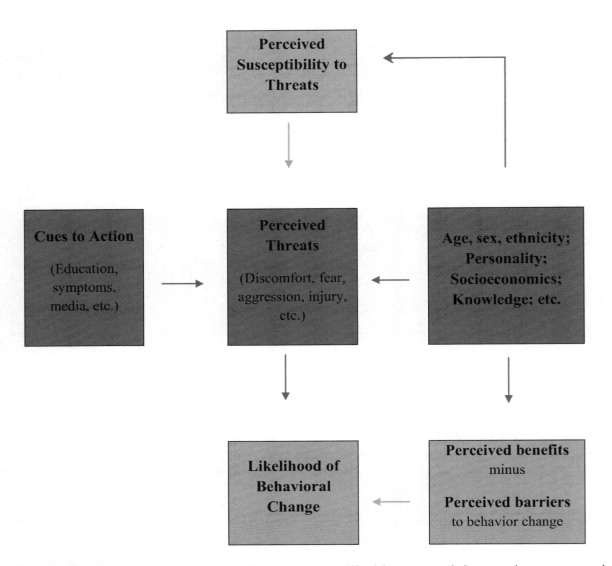

Perceived threats are those fears that exercise will either cause injury or increase a pain that already exists. You must be aware of your clients' fears. Move slowly at first. Never try to push clients to do too much too soon.

Perceived benefits are the benefits of exercise that a client is aware of. These benefits are well-documented, but it is a health fitness professional's responsibility to educate clients about how exercise can directly improve their overall health and any personal fitness challenges they have. People value medical opinions, so seek support from the client's physician if possible.

Perceived barriers are the reasons people give for not exercising regularly. Many people feel they don't have the time, funds, or physical abilities to exercise. You must listen to your clients' concerns and work with them to develop ways around any barriers.

Changing Behavior
Behavior change occurs in stages. The **Trans-theoretical Model of Change in Behavior** (TMC) is a model illustrating the six stages of change that people go through when developing new patterns of behavior. These stages, listed below, explain how levels of both willingness to change and motivation vary with progress.

1. **Pre-Contemplation**: The first stage of TMC. In this stage, a person is not open to making lifestyle changes and is possibly in denial of the fact that any modifications are needed. Often, because it is challenging to help clients in this stage change their behavior, various modes of media advertisements are used to help raise exercise awareness.

2. **Contemplation**: The stage wherein people begin to consider making healthy changes. They haven't taken any steps toward making a change, but they've developed the intention to do so. People in this stage often make resolutions to begin exercising on or right after a certain date, such as the first day of a new year or a milestone birthday.

3. **Preparation**: In the **preparation** stage, people actually make an effort to put a fitness plan in motion. They may sign up for a class, join a gym, or purchase athletic gear, but they have not yet adopted new fitness-oriented behaviors.

4. **Action**: This is the fourth and most critical stage of change, in which people begin activities and programs. Their receiving ongoing encouragement and direction is crucial at this point, because many people become discouraged when changes do not occur as immediately as they had hoped. As a result, the Action stage sees a high rate of drop-out, so health fitness professionals need to be as proactive as possible.

    Try working with clients to establish specific short term goals in order to show progress. For example: set measurable goals, like losing a certain number of pounds or increasing the number of repetitions per machine by a specific amount. You can even set one-time goals for clients to work on between sessions, such as not snacking after dinner for two days in a row.

    These goals are more readily attainable, and therefore empowering to your client. Be sure to provide specific verbal praise when clients show improvement (and even point out their progress in areas other than weight loss). Let clients know that you believe in them!

The SMART System of Goal-Setting Can Ensure Success	
Specific	Detail a set desire.
Measurement	Establish a tangible goal.
Action-Oriented	Name the planned steps to success.
Realistic	Keep it doable!
Timed	Establish a realistic time frame.

5. **Maintenance**: The stage in which people have achieved a higher, maintainable level of fitness and adopted a lifestyle that supports continued health. They are now maintaining this healthy behavior.

6. **Termination**: Remains possible even for people who fluctuate between the Action and Maintenance stages. As the name suggests, people in this stage quit, or terminate, the program. To prevent termination and to keep clients focused on fitness goals and moving through the stages of change, it is essential for health fitness professionals to use motivational strategies, support, and rewards to match their clients' current positions.

Educate your clients about how using cues can keep them focused. Cues can be anything that reminds a client to stay on the fitness track; for example, post-it note motivational quotes on mirrors.

Processes of Behavioral Change
Within the **Trans-theoretical Model of Change** are ten processes called the Processes of Behavioral Change. Five of these are cognitive processes most effective when used during the initial stages of change. The other five are behavioral processes, more useful during the Action and Maintenance stages.

The Five Cognitive Processes:

1. The first cognitive process is **Consciousness Raising**. This can consist of marketing strategies such as special offers for gym memberships, or advertisements about the benefits of good nutrition and the health risks associated with inactivity.

2. **Dramatic Relief** includes using strategies such as psychodrama, grieving losses, and role playing in order to experience and express feelings about a problem preventing exercise.

3. **Environmental Reevaluation** targets specific habits. For example: If targeting smoking, you would provide the client with information about the dangers associated with direct and second-hand smoke.

4. **Self-Reevaluation** occurs when a fitness novice's knowledge and understanding of exercise's benefits increases; at that point, she gains motivation. Health fitness professionals can begin educating new clients about the health gains associated with higher fitness levels during the Preparation stage.

5. **Social Liberation** is the final cognitive process through which people realize that increased health and fitness levels open up opportunities that weren't previously available.

The Five Behavioral Processes:

1. **Counterconditioning** involves the replacement of an unwanted habitual behavior with a healthier alternative. From a fitness standpoint, the unwanted behavior is a habit that keeps someone from achieving improved health.
     For example, a client often forgoes his 5 p.m. workout because he forgets to bring sweatpants to the office. In this scenario, his personal trainer can suggest places to go walking in professional attire. This option keeps the client engaged in something active.

2. **Helping Relationships** promote supportive social bonds, possibly with other health club members, as a means to staying on task with fitness.

3. **Reinforcement Management** provides a reward for good behavior, which reinforces that good behavior. With exercise, the health benefits tend to serve as the reward for people who have already adopted an active lifestyle. However, for clients who are still progressing through the initial stages of change, personal trainers need to use more immediate forms of positive reinforce. For example, offer specific verbal praise when a client shows improvement in form

4. **Self-Liberation** occurs during the final stages of change, when people discover a love for a particular exercise or activity and then make it a permanent part of their routine. It is a personal trainer's duty to help clients discover activities that are enjoyable and rewarding enough to become habits.

5. **Stimulus control** means removing anything that supports the reoccurrence of a bad habit. For instance, giving away the cookie jar if cutting sugar from your diet.

Decisional Balance is another component of the Trans-theoretical Model of Change. This part of the model, from a fitness perspective, looks at how people view the pros and cons of a healthy lifestyle as they move through the stages of change. In the beginning, the cons outweigh the pros, but this balance reverses by the time they reach the final stage (Maintenance).

Self-Efficacy is synonymous with self-confidence. We'll cover it in greater detail below.

Behavioral Strategies to Enhance Physical Activity Participation and Health

Social Cognitive Theory
Social Cognitive Theory identifies and explains the reciprocal interaction of behavioral, personal, and environmental influences and the way this interaction creates unique behavior patterns. The Social Cognitive Theory focuses on the idea of a reciprocal dynamic involving personal, behavioral and environmental influences—in other words, people influence and are influenced by their environments.

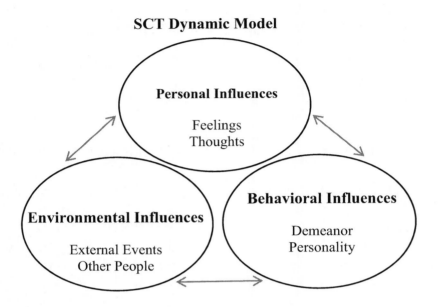

SCT Dynamic Model

This three-way dynamic reciprocal relationship creates unique realities for every individual, because each part is intrinsically tied to the others. People's thoughts, feelings, beliefs, demeanors, and life experiences all affect the way they view and comprehend events taking place around them.

These events, or environmental influences, are likewise shaped by the actions of the people who are present. For example, a person with a strong personality and a person with a reserved demeanor will most likely have different experiences in similar circumstances. They will evoke different attitudes from the people around them and, as a result, observe different results.

Key Constructs of SCT:

    1. Observational Learning.

    2. Reinforcement.

    3. Self-Efficacy.

When people observe others receiving rewards for certain actions, the observers are likely to partake in the same behavior. For example: A young child sees that her older sister receives praise for clearing her plate. Wanting to receive praise as well, the young child also clears her plate. This is the main thrust of **Observational Learning**, which emphasizes the importance of having positive role models who consistently demonstrate the benefits of fitness.

Likewise, positive **Reinforcement** is essential for someone who is on their way to making exercise a permanent practice. Health fitness professionals can initially be the sole providers of positive reinforcement, so it is important to help clients in the early stages of change to feel good about small accomplishments.

The most important component of SCT from a fitness stand point is **Self-Efficacy**. When a person has self-efficacy, they know they have all the knowledge they need to confidently walk into any health club. Health fitness professionals must equip their clients with the knowledge and support they need to achieve this level of confidence. There are many ways to do this, but some basic ideas can be: informing clients how to adjust seats, change weight loads, and program cardio equipment; letting a client know what to expect when walking into a new environment; or even walking them through the steps they'll be taking in their program to improve confidence.

Another important aspect of helping clients gain self-efficacy is simply acknowledging and addressing their fears and doubts. To do this, effective health fitness professionals must hone their **active listening** skills so their clients feel important, safe, and understood. Active listening means that the focus is completely on the speaker. As active listeners, health fitness professionals must have open body language, make direct eye contact, and ensure that no unnecessary multitasking takes place. Also, it is important for health fitness professionals to not be assuming they already know what clients are about to say or thinking about a response before clients have finished speaking.

Be sure not to interrupt clients while they are speaking, but do use gestures and facial expressions that relay understanding, such as nodding, to show you are actively listening. Lastly, allow a pause at the end of the conversation to make sure clients have finished and then paraphrase back main points for clarification.

Feedback and Reinforcement Methods
Feedback is an important way to let clients know they have your attention. More importantly, specific positive feedback is an effective tool for keeping clients motivated during the initial stages of change.

Extrinsic rewards are tangible items such as free t-shirts or training sessions after clients complete an established goal.

These extrinsic rewards work well in the early stages, but trainers need to help clients realize **intrinsic rewards** for prolonged success. Intrinsic rewards are the benefits that come when clients attain a higher level of fitness. The improved health and wellness at this point serve as the rewards that inspire permanent success.

Exercise Barriers and Exercise Motivations: How to Approach Them

Exercise barriers, also called **perceived barriers**, are the reasons people give for not exercising. Most commonly, people feel that exercise is impossible due to time, monetary, or physical constraints. Listen to your clients' concerns and work with them to develop ways around the barriers.

Exercise motivators, on the other hand, are factors which have inspired your client to exercise. Typically, these involve improvements in health and physical appearance. It is important to note to your client that these results are not instantaneous. Educate your client about how exercise can directly improve their overall health. During the critical period (the first three-to-six months), personal trainers need to use more immediate forms of positive reinforcement. Offering specific verbal praise when a client shows improvement is one way to nurture motivation. People also value medical opinions, so get the support of the client's physician when possible.

Client Expectations

You must help your clients set realistic, measurable goals in the initial stage of an exercise program. When clients expect too much too soon, they often become frustrated, or they try to exercise beyond their current level of fitness. This can lead to a dropout. Prevent this outcome by helping to create specific short-term goals.

> For example, if a client says she wants to lose weight, a trainer can establish how many pounds to lose in a specific time period. Shorter goals which may seems unrelated can also help take the focus off of weight loss. Have her commit to drinking a healthy amount of water over the weekend – or perhaps tell her to try not drinking soda for two days. (Tea is a great alternative for those who drink soda for the caffeine.) Such reachable goals provide constant encouragement and elevation of self-esteem, making those larger goals seem more attainable.

Client's Attitude towards Personal Fitness

Many people find physical activity draining – some people have related exercising to a chore, or even torture! This is not desirable at all; you obviously want your client to have an enjoyable experience in order to increase program adherence. Find out what kinds of activities they like or dislike. A client who severely dislikes weight-lifting, but enjoys dancing, may respond to coordinated aerobic classes such as kickboxing or Zumba.

Questionnaires can provide a wealth of information about **determining factors** of a client's attitude. Some examples of determining factors include demographic background, family status, current level of health, and exercise history.

Determining factors play a combined role in forming a person's belief system, behavior, and attitude toward change.

A client's readiness for behavior change depends greatly on their motivation. Encourage clients to discuss what health benefits they hope to achieve, and what they expect from you. The information gathered from their verbal and non-verbal communication can provide clues. Also, learn their physical and physiological limitations, as well as preferences.

As well-versed as you may be in gathering information, you also must understand the best **delivery method** for providing information *to* clients. Everyone has a preferred way of receiving information. The three basic information pathways are **visual, auditory,** and **kinesthetic**.

Visual Learners benefit the most from visual aids. Bring diagrams, or incorporate posters, when providing information. If you are describing the best kinds of exercise gear to use, pull up some pictures to use for examples, or bring in equipment for demonstrations.

Demonstrations are also useful for **kinesthetic learners** – those who receive information best when it is incorporated with an action. This type of learning is also called **tactile**. Again, having visual aids which the client can touch will help them absorb information more fully. For example: Bring in a replica of five pounds worth of fat. Have your client hold it to gauge its weight or see how it feels.

Auditory Learners, on the other hand, are the **listeners**. They respond best when instructions are spoken or detailed. For example: If you provide a handout detailing the different levels of fitness, an auditory learner would benefit from your walking them through each point, giving them the chance to ask for clarification.

You can identify your clients' learning preferences by watching for verbal and non-verbal clues during initial meetings and subsequent training sessions. For instance, clients who look closely at visual aids posted on work-stations most likely have a dominant visual pathway and will require a demonstration of skills. Conversely, clients who listen intently to verbal instructions, but rarely refer to the visual aids, probably prefer auditory input. Kinesthetic learners typically understand an exercise fully only after having completed a set or two.

OBTAINING INFORMATION

A successful relationship between a client and personal trainer begins with the gathering of valuable information during the initial screening process to determine if the health status of a client and goals are matched with the trainer. Based on the information gathered, it may be necessary to refer the client to a medical professional for clearance or permission to exercise and/or strength train. The need for medical clearance should not be a deterrent as almost everyone can engage in some form of exercise.

Administration: Administering a proper physiological assessment helps the personal trainer identify any medical conditions that may put a client at risk, assist in designing a program with appropriate modifications, and fulfill any legal insurance requirements for both the personal trainer and the fitness center.

Reporting: The health background of any client is the primary tool used by personal trainers to set up a safe and effective exercise program.

Obtaining this information is as simple as asking a few questions in writing on a form. Ask clients if they currently have or have a history of:

- Heart problems.

- High blood pressure.

- Diabetes.

- High cholesterol.

- Lung disease.

- Discomfort in their chest, neck or jaw during physical exercise or exertion.

- Chest pain, dizziness or extreme shortness of breath during physical exercise or exertion.

- Any injuries or disorders in the back, joints, or muscles that may be exacerbated by physical exercise or exertion.

You should also ask whether they have any immediate family with heart problems; whether or not they smoke; what, if any, chronic illnesses they may suffer from or have suffered from in the past; whether or not they already exercise regularly; if a doctor has ever restricted their physical exercise; if they take any medications (and, if so, which ones); and, in the case of women, if they are or recently have been pregnant.

Termination Criteria: If a client answers "yes" to any of these questions, then they should obtain clearance from their doctor. A doctor's release reduces the personal trainer's liability, minimizes the client's risk and enables the doctor to give specific instructions for their patient's exercise program. A client should be terminated from personal training services if the anticipated goals or expected outcomes have been achieved, or if the client is unable to continue training for personal reasons.

Pretest Considerations for Health Appraisal

Health fitness professionals must be both well-trained and knowledgeable in client-health risk appraisal, a systematic approach in screening clients for: signs and symptoms, a family history of, and risk factors for disease. New clients, especially, will need to fill out and use a variety of forms. Information drawn from the screening can help identify:

- Contraindications to exercise. In the presence of contraindications, the health fitness professional should determine whether or not the client may still participate in an exercise program.

- Individuals who must undergo additional exercise testing—and even a medical evaluation—because of an increased risk for disease due to age, symptoms, and/or additional risk factors.

- Those who should participate only in medically-supervised exercise programs, due to the presence of a clinically significant disease.

- Any other person who may have special considerations.

In the presence of any of the above, clients would require a medical evaluation before engaging in a fitness program. They may even need medical supervision while exercising.

Informed Consent

Before any exercise testing or health appraisals can begin, patients must provide a form which indicates their own informed consent. (An example can be found on the following page.) This form stresses the risks and benefits of exercise testing and programming, while stating those occurrences which are possible during testing, such as risks, side effects, etc.

Clients must always be fully aware of testing or exercise procedures and their risks; the signed informed consent form serves as both a legal and ethical document in these regards.

INFORMED CONSENT

I hereby consent to participate in the outpatient exercise at _____.

I understand that I will be placed on a program of graded exercise and activities. The levels of exercise I will do will be based on my cardiovascular response. Regularly scheduled sessions will be held for the purpose of evaluating my progress. Explicit instructions regarding the amount and kind of exercises and activities I should do will be provided. My daily exercise program will be based on my pulse rate response and level of exertion during the treatment sessions.

I understand that there exists a possibility of certain changes during the exercise session. These changes include abnormal blood pressure, heart dysrhythmias, fainting, and in very rare circumstances heart attack or even death. I understand that every effort will be made to minimize these problems by obtaining a thorough medical history and observations during the exercise sessions.

I realize it is necessary for me to promptly report to the exercise physiologist any signs or symptoms indicating discomfort or distress. I consent to the administration of any immediate resuscitation measures deemed advisable by the supervisor of the exercise session and/or any other qualified medical personnel present at the time.

No assurance has been given to me that this rehabilitation program will increase my functional activity level. The results may help in evaluating what types of activity I may carry out safely in my daily life.

I have read and understand the above information. Any questions which have arisen have been answered to my satisfaction.

Participant signature_____ Date_____

Witness signature_____ Date_____

PAR-Q

An effective, safe, and commonly-used form for screening is the **Physical Activity Readiness Questionnaire (PAR-Q)** form. The PAR-Q has been recommended as a minimal standard for entry into moderate-intensity exercise programs; it was designed to identify the small number of adults for whom physical activity might be inappropriate or who should receive medical advice concerning the most suitable type of activity. It may be obtained from the American College of Sports Medicine.

The PAR-Q requires clients to fill out a seven-question questionnaire regarding their health. The questions ask:

- Has the client ever been diagnosed with a heart condition and told by a doctor to engage in doctor-recommended physical exercise only?

- Does the client feel chest pain during physical activity?

- Has the client felt chest pain at rest during the past month?

- Has the client recently experienced dizziness, loss of balance, or loss of consciousness?

- Does the client have a bone or joint problem that may be exacerbated by physical activity?

- Is the client currently prescribed medication for blood pressure or cardiovascular conditions?

- Does the client know of any other reason that physical activity may be a risk?

If a client answers "yes" to any of the questions on the form, then you are required to obtain a consent form (also known as a **Medical Release** form) from that client's healthcare provider before beginning an exercise program. All clients must also sign the **Informed Consent** and **Release of Liability** forms, which are often combined into a single form.

You may or may not, depending on the client, require the completion of other forms to add specificity and coherency to a client's profile. These can include: Orthopedic History, Nutritional Profile, Past and Current Activity History, Exercise Attitude Questionnaire, etc.

The information gathered in the screening is used by health fitness professionals for a variety of purposes: making recommendations for lifestyle modifications, suggesting strategies for exercise testing, prescribing exercise prescriptions, etc.

Physician Referral

As you will see, The PAR-Q states that clients should obtain medical clearance from their physician prior to starting an exercise program. This is a safeguard for high-risk clients who may compromise their health by exercising in a facility without medically-trained staff and necessary equipment.

Some patients may indicate a risk or contraindication to testing. In those cases, you need to refer your patient to their physician for further testing specifically regarding those contraindications. This is mandatory for further clinical testing, as well as for when the client requires medical clearance into an office- or hospital-based program (or medical fitness center).

The physician can provide a formal referral form, or simply a doctor's office script with the physician's name, stating the diagnosis and exercise prescription.

ACSM Risk Stratification

The PAR-Q is a quick form which, though effective, covers general information. A more comprehensive process of determining a patient's risk is through the ACSM Risk Stratification method. **Risk stratification** assigns individuals to low, medium, or high risk, based on presence of conditions. We will go over how to recognize the conditions, signs, and symptoms of various disease states later in this chapter.

The American College of Sports Medicine has a comprehensive approach in identifying any risk factors that your client might have: the **ACSM Risk Stratification Matrix**, which makes recommendations based upon the category (Low, Moderate, or High Risk) into which your client falls.

ACSM Risk Stratification is determined by adding up the number of risk factors indicated by clients during their screenings.

Positive Risk Factors

- **Family History of Disease**: Myocardial infarction, coronary revascularization, or sudden death before the age of 55 (for male first-degree relatives) or 65 (female first-degree relatives) years of age.

- **Cigarette Smoking**: Includes those with a current smoking habit, as well as those who have recently (within six months) quit and those who have been exposed to second-hand smoke for over six months.

- **Hypertension**: Those currently taking antihypertensive medication, and/or those who have a confirmed (by at least two separate measurements on two separate occasions) systolic blood pressure $\geq$ 140 mm Hg or diastolic $\geq$ 90 mm Hg.

- **Hypercholesterolemia/Dyslipidemia**: Those currently taking lipid-lowering medication, and/or those with a total serum cholesterol > 200 mg/dL (5.2 mmol/L), or high-density lipoprotein cholesterol of .35 mg/dL (0.9 mmol/L).[1]

- **Impaired Fasting Glucose**: A fasting blood glucose$\geq$ 110 mg/dL (6.1 mmol/L, confirmed by at least two separate measurements on two separate occasions).

- **Obesity**: BMI $\geq$ 30 mg/m^2, or a waist girth exceeding approximately 39.4 inches.

- **Sedentary Lifestyle**: Those not meeting the recommended amount of physical activity as provided by the U.S. Surgeon General's Report. Typical Recommendation: At least 30 minutes of physical activity at a moderate intensity (40 – 60% VO2), at least three days a weeks, for at least three months.

---

[1] Low-density lipoprotein cholesterol measurement is preferred over total cholesterol.

Negative Risk Factors

- **High Serum HDL Cholesterol**: > 60 mg/dL (1.6 mmol/L).

Emerging Risk Factors

- **Inflammatory Markers**: i.e., Reactive C Protein (CRP) and fibrinogen.

Once you've ascertained the amount of indications to any of the above given by your client, you may then classify them into one of the three categories, which also depend on the client's age:

- **Low Risk**: Men < 45 years of age and women < 55 years of age, who are asymptomatic while meeting no more than one risk factor.

- **Moderate Risk**: Men > 45 years and women > 55 years, or those who meet the threshold for two or more risk factors.

- **High Risk**: Individuals with one or more signs and symptoms listed or a known cardiovascular, pulmonary, or metabolic disease.

These categories also come in handy for determining an appropriate level of exercise testing.

ACSM Recommendations for (A) Current Medical Examination[2] & Exercise Testing Prior to Participation and (B) Physician Supervision of Exercise Tests

	Low Risk	Moderate Risk	High Risk
A. Moderate Exercise	Not Necessary	Not Necessary	Recommended
Vigorous Exercise	Not Necessary	Recommended	Recommended
B. Submaximal Test	Not Necessary	Not Necessary	Recommended
Maximal Test	Not Necessary	Recommended	Recommended

Alternatively, you can classify your patient according to these categories:

- **Low Risk**: Assumed when each of the below is present.
  - No significant LVD (EF > 50%).
  - No resting or exercised-induced complex dysrhythmias.
  - No complications with any of the following: MI, CABG, PTCA, atherectomy, and/or stent.
    - Absence of CHF or signs/symptoms indicating post-event ischemia.
  - Normal hemodynamics with exercise and recovery.
  - Patient is asymptomatic, which includes the absence of angina with exertion or recovery.
  - Function capacity ≥ METS (if n/a, don't use FWC to determine risk).
  - Absence of clinical depression.

---

[2] Within the Past Year

- **Moderate Risk**: Assumed for patients classified as neither highest nor lowest risk.
  - Moderately-impaired LV function (EF = 40 – 50%).
  - Angina signs and symptoms during moderate levels of exercise (5 – 6.9 METs) or during recovery.
  - Those with abnormal resting EKGs, including: LBBB; LVH, with or without resting ST-T changes; non-specific intraventricular conduction delays; WPW; and ventricular paced rhythms.
  - Those on digitalis therapy.
  - Those with tests negative for ischemia who fail to achieve 85% of maximal predicted heart rate.

- **High Risk**: Assumed with the presence of any one of the risk factors included in this category.
  - Decreased LV function (EF < 40%).
  - Survivor of cardiac arrest or sudden death.
  - Complex ventricular dysrhythmia, at rest or with exercise.
  - MI or cardiac surgery complicated by cardiogenic shock, CHF, and/or signs and symptoms of post-procedure ischemia.
  - Abnormal hemodynamics with exercise (especially flat or decreasing SBP or chronotropic incompetence with increasing workload).
  - Signs and symptoms indicating angina pectoris at low levels of exercise (< 5.0 METs) or in recovery.
  - Function capacity < 5.0 METs (if FWC n/a, don't use this variable to consider risk).
  - Clinically-significant depression.

ASSESSMENTS

While almost anyone can exercise safely, some people may benefit from an exercise consultation. The top two reasons to get exercise prescriptions are safety and efficiency. An exercise program needs to be designed specifically for health status, goals, abilities, and interests. When working with clients who are healthy, you will generally only need informed consent before developing exercise prescriptions for them; each exercise program will need to suit the client's current fitness level.

When performing exercise testing for a patient, ACSM has certain steps, which can be put into the acronym "M.R.I.P.L."

"M" – Medical History
Ascertain the client's medical history through a series of questionnaires helps determine the following: the client's needs, special or otherwise; the necessity for a more extensive medical evaluation; and/or if the client ought to be referred to a different facility.

If clients end up staying at your facility, then you must also determine whether or not they have a clinical history which warrants modifying the typical prescription/program.

"R" – Risk Factor Assessment
The client needs to fill out a risk factor assessment form, identifying any health risk factors which would require a physician's approval before beginning a program. We will cover risk factors in greater depth later on, as well.

"I" – Interpreting the Data
At this stage, you should begin thinking about how best to design the client's exercise program. Once the client has completed their medical history and risk factor assessment forms, you must then assess the quality and completeness of the **fitness assessment**. At the clearance of their physician, the client will need to perform a fitness assessment, which should cover all **five components of fitness**:

1. Cardiovascular endurance.

2. Muscular strength.

3. Muscular endurance.

4. Flexibility.

5. Body composition.

We'll go into more detail regarding the fitness assessment later on in the chapter.

Interpreting the data from this and the previous steps will help determine the client's health status, as well as identify specific goals and hurdles which ought to be considered in their exercise prescription.

"P" – Prescribing an Exercise Program
Now, you can develop your client's complete exercise prescription, appropriate for his or her current fitness level, which achieves a balance between goals and needs.

"L" – Lifestyle Counseling
This is perhaps one of the most important steps, which changes the exercise prescription from a temporary fix to the ideal: a lifestyle change. The client must be informed of the rationale underlying the developed program. Review all the information from the previous M.R.I.P. steps in detail with your client; then discuss specific lifestyle changes he or she can make, integrating suggested changes in diet, exercise regiment, and CVD risk factor reduction. Be as thorough and clear as possible. As appropriate for the individual client, include the following specific directions for:

1. Modifying risk factors for cardiovascular disease, including changes in diet and exercise habits.

2. Beginning a goal-oriented exercise program.
   - Provide modifications in CV exercises for clients as appropriate to their clinical and exercise history.
   - Include dietary changes in keeping with USDA Dietary Guidelines, the Therapeutic Lifestyle Change Diet, and/or the Food Guide Pyramid in weight loss plans.
   - Consider the client's clinical and exercise history when designing programs of restrictive exercise.

3. Referring clients to specialists as necessary: references may include dietitians or nutritionists for assistance in modifying diets or developing new dietary habits; physicians for consultations or medical prescriptions; and counselors to provide assistance in stress management, smoking cessation, or other lifestyle changes.

Fitness Assessment: Risk Factors and Contraindications

In order to identify any underlying health issues which would limit a client's ability to exercise, a well-trained health fitness professional will usually require the client to undergo a general physical exam by their physician. Once the physician gives clearance, an appropriate exercise program can start being developed.

In the meantime, you may offer your client a fitness assessment, or exercise testing, in order to determine his or her baseline fitness level and what exercise is safe for the client to perform.

An assessment often includes simple measurements of blood pressure and heart rate, as well as strength, flexibility (sit and reach test), body mass index (BMI), girth measurements, body fat percentage, cardiovascular endurance (3-minute step test), exercise history, and concludes with the client's own goals and interests. A graded exercise test, or **stress test**, will usually only be recommended by a physician if the client has symptoms of coronary artery diseases, or significant risk factors for CAD.

A screening tool, such as a **Par-Q** or **Health Status Questionnaire** (HSQ), may be used to quickly and accurately identify the following: medical contraindications to exercise, risk factors for coronary heart disease, and lifestyle behaviors which may affect your client's ability to exercise safely.

Risk Factors

Disease states like cardiovascular disease (CVD), stroke, Type II diabetes mellitus (T2DM), hypertension (HTN), breast cancer, obesity, anxiety, depression, colon cancer, and more have an inverse relationship with physical activity.

In individuals with normal cardiovascular systems, exercise does not provoke cardiovascular events. However, in certain individuals, vigorous exercise may result in cardiac arrest, or even sudden death. These individuals would have diagnosed or present cardiovascular diseases, congenital abnormalities, and/or hereditary abnormalities, such as:

- Hypertrophic cardiomyopathy.
- Coronary artery abnormalities (such as vessels that are abnormally narrow).
- Aortic stenosis.

Because of the prevalence of cardiac events in those populations, it is absolutely essential to screen for the presence of signs, symptoms, and risk factors of heart disease and other conditions.

The three most looked-for diseases – cardiovascular, pulmonary, and metabolic – include the following:

1. **Cardiovascular Diseases**: All cardiac, peripheral (PAD), vascular, and/or cerebrovascular diseases.

2. **Pulmonary Diseases**: Chronic obstructive pulmonary disease (COPD), asthma, interstitial lining disease, and/or cystic fibrosis.

3. **Metabolic Diseases**: Diabetes mellitus (Type I or II), thyroid disorders, renal disease, and/or liver disease. Symptoms can include: high blood sugar levels (sign of Diabetes Mellitus and obesity); shakiness and disorientation (symptoms of hypoglycemia); weight gain, sluggish behavior, and hair loss (indicative of hypothyroidism)

The signs and symptoms of cardiovascular and pulmonary diseases include:

- Pain, discomfort, distress, or the equivalent, in areas which may be due to ischemia. Such areas include: chest, neck, jaw, arms, etc.

- Shortness of breath occurring at rest or with mild exertion.

- Dizziness or syncope.

- Edema, especially of the ankle.

- Tachycardia, or other arrhythmic occurrences such as a known heart murmur.

- Orthopnea or paroxysmal dyspnea.

- Intermittent claudication.

- Unusual fatigue or shortness of breath with usual activities of daily life.

Aside from the big three, you must be familiar with the following conditions and their typical symptoms:

Angina
Heart Pain.

Symptoms Include: (Severity, type, and duration can vary.) Chest pain or discomfort; pain in arms, neck, jaw, shoulder, or back (accompanying chest pain); nausea; fatigue; shortness of breath; anxiety; sweating; and dizziness.

- **Stable Angina** is triggered by physical exertion or mental/emotional stress; it dissipates with rest. Angina feels like indigestion; pain may spread to the back, arms, or other areas. This is the most common type of angina.

- **Unstable Angina** may signal a heart attack and is a medical emergency. It can occur when the victim is at rest and is more severe and longer-lasting than stable angina—pain may last for up to thirty minutes.

Arrhythmias
Abnormal heart rhythm.

- **Tachycardia**: Very fast heart rate.

- **Bradycardia**: Unusually slow heart rate.

- **Atrial Fibrillation**: Irregular heart rhythm.

- **Ventricular Ectopic Beats (VEB)**: A heart beat arising from an abnormal focus. These are called premature (occurring before the scheduled next beat) or escape (occurring later than the scheduled next beat) beats.

Dyspnea

Shortness of Breath (SOB). Difficult or uncomfortable breathing experienced subjectively (perceived and reported by patient). Dyspnea can occur at rest or be caused by exertion.

Exertion-caused Dyspnea suggests presence of cardiopulmonary disorders (especially left ventricular dysfunction or chronic obstructive pulmonary disease). Dyspnea should be differentiated from the following, which are indicative of respiratory variations that are not subjective:

- **Tachypnea**: Increase in respiratory rate above normal.

- **Hyperventilation**: Increased minute ventilation relative to metabolic need.

- **Hyperpnea**: Disproportionate rise in minute ventilation relative to an increase in metabolic level.

Important Note: Dyspnea on Exertion (DOE) may occur normally.

Edema

Edema is swelling caused by excess fluid trapped in the body's tissues. It commonly occurs in the arms, hands, legs, ankles, and feet. Medication can be taken to remove excess fluid, and removing salt from the patient's diet typically relieves the swelling. However, edema can be a sign of an underlying disease (heart failure, kidney disease, cirrhosis of the liver, etc.).

Symptoms Include: Swelling or puffiness of the tissue directly under the skin, increased abdominal size, skin that appears stretched and/or shiny, and/or skin which retains a dimple after being pressed for several seconds.

- **Unilateral Edema**: A limb which is completely swollen. Often results from venous thrombosis or lymphatic blockage in the limb.

- **Ankle Edema**: Most commonly-seen edema. A characteristic sign of heart failure or bilateral chronic venous insufficiency.

Heart Murmur

A heart murmur may be caused by blood flow through an overworked or damaged heart valve; while usually harmless, this may indicate valvular abnormalities.

Intermittent Claudication

Intermittent claudication is pain that occurs when a muscle lacking adequate blood supply is stressed by exercise. It is intensified when walking at an incline, and may occur on an ongoing basis, but does not occur during standing or sitting.

Symptoms include a cramp-like feeling that may disappear within a few minutes after exercise.

Orthopnea: Orthopnea is difficulty breathing when reclining. It usually indicates LV dysfunction.

Paroxysmal Nocturnal Dyspnea (PND)
Dyspnea which occurs usually after one or two hours of sleep.

Symptoms Include: Wheezing and coughing, which waken the sleeper. Can occur in COPDs. Oftentimes, the sleeper is relieved once awakening to either sit up or productively cough.

Syncope
Loss of consciousness, usually caused by reduced perfusion to the brain. When accompanied by dizziness, syncope may result from cardiac disorders preventing normal cardiac output. These disorders include severe CAD, hypertrophic cardiomyopathy, aortic stenosis, and malignant ventricular dysrhythmias. Dizziness may also occur from loss of venous return to the heart.

Palpitations
Feelings of fluttering, rapid, or pounding heartbeats. Usually harmless, these can be triggered by: stress, exercise, or medication. However, palpitations may signify a greater cardiac disorder.

Symptoms Include: Perceived feelings of skipped, fluttering, too fast, or pounding heartbeats. These can occur at any time—active or resting—and can be felt in the throat, neck, and/or chest. If they are accompanied by chest discomfort/pain, fainting, shortness of breath, and/or severe dizziness, then seek emergency medical attention.

Contraindications and Indications

Before performing an exercise test, you must first identify your client's indications/contraindications. In medicine or fitness, indications and contraindications are very important when determining risk factors that could put your client in an unsafe environment.

An **indication** is a valid reason to use certain tests, medications, procedures, etc.

The opposite are **contraindications**: conditions or factors requiring the withholding of certain medical treatments or tests.

Contraindications to Exercise Testing
These are things to look out for *before* beginning a test. Absolute contraindications demand that, under no circumstances, should the test be performed. Relative contraindications call for concern; however the test may still be performed, though sometimes with modifications.

Absolute
- Acute myocardial infarction (within two days).
- Unstable angina, not previously stabilized by medical therapy.
- Uncontrolled cardiac arrhythmias, causing symptoms or hemodynamic compromise.
- Symptomatic severe aortic stenosis.
- Uncontrolled symptomatic heart failure.
- Acute pulmonary embolus or pulmonary infarction.

- Acute myocarditis or pericarditis.
- Acute aortic dissection.
- Suspected or known dissection aneurysm.
- Acute system infection, accompanied by fever, body aches, or swollen lymph glands.

Relative
- Left main coronary stenosis.
- Moderate stenotic valvular heart disease.
- Electrolyte abnormalities, such as hypokalemia or hypomagnesaemia.
- Severe arterial hypertension (greater than 200 mmHg and/or diastolic BP greater than 110 mmHg at rest).
- Tachyarrhythmias or bradyarrhythmias.
- Hypertrophic cardiomyopathy and/or other forms of outflow tract obstruction.
- Neuromuscular, musculoskeletal, or rheumatoid disorders that could be exacerbated by exercise. Symptoms can include: high sensitivity to hot or cold temperatures; lower extremity muscle weakness; foot drop; loss of sensation and/or balance/coordination; and tremors of varying degrees.
- Ventricular aneurysm.
- Uncontrolled metabolic disease, such as diabetes, thyrotoxicosis, or myxedema.
- Chronic infectious diseases such as mononucleosis, hepatitis, or AIDS.
- Mental or physical impairment leading to inability to exercise adequately.
- High-degree atrioventricular block.

Absolute Indications
During testing, immediately terminate the testing if you suspect any of the following:

- Myocardial or acute myocardial infarction (heart attack).
- Poor perfusion (circulation/blood flow): indications include a pale appearance (pallor), cyanosis (turning blue), or cold and clammy skin.
- Vertigo (illusory dizzying movement), ataxia (lack of coordination) visual problems, confusion, or other symptoms of CNS (central nervous system) problems.
- Drop in blood pressure
- Onset of moderate-to-severe angina (chest pain).
- Serious abnormal heart rhythms (arrhythmias) increasing premature ventricular contractions, atrial fibrillation with fast ventricular response, including sustained ventricular tachycardia, or second or third degree AV block.
- Any inability to monitor the ECG.
- Client's request to stop.

Relative Indications
These indicate that special attention ought to be paid to the exercise testing, to look for increasing reasons to halt the test. Like red flags, they bring attention to the specific problem. However, unlike *absolute* indications, they do not call for the immediate termination of the test.

- Increasing chest pain.
- Physical or verbal manifestations of shortness of breath or severe fatigue.
  - Wheezing.

- Leg cramps or intermittent claudication (grade 3 on a 4-point scale).
- Hypertensive response (SBP >260 mm Hg; DBP>115 mm Hg).
- Pronounced ECG changes from baseline 1>2 mm of horizontal or down sloping ST-segment depression, or >2 mm of ST-segment elevation (except in a VR).
- Exercise-induced bundle branch block that cannot be distinguished from ventricular tachycardia.
- Less-serious arrhythmias such as supraventricular tachycardia.

Fitness Assessment: Five Components of Fitness

Once you have appropriately gauged the indications/contraindications/risk factors for your client, you may begin (with the clearance of a physician, when necessary) the fitness assessment. As stated before, the fitness assessment is comprised of **five components of fitness**: Cardiovascular Endurance; Muscular Strength; Muscular Endurance; Flexibility; and Body Composition.

Cardiovascular Endurance
Cardiovascular endurance (fitness), or cardiorespiratory fitness, is often considered the most important aspect of a client's total fitness; the ability to perform large-muscle dynamic, moderate-to-high intensity exercise for prolonged periods depends upon cardiovascular fitness.

A measure of the heart's ability to pump oxygen-rich blood to all the working muscles in the human body is one way to gauge cardiovascular fitness. If the heart is kept healthy, then the risk of numerous health problems is significantly reduced.

Low cardiovascular fitness in individuals markedly increases the risk of premature death by all causes, especially cardiovascular disease.

There are many ways of measuring cardiovascular endurance, from VO2 Max tests, to the Bruce test. We'll detail some of the more commonly-used ones here.

- **ECG:** Cardiovascular Endurance can be measured in a hospital setting, where a physician monitors an exercise (stress) test (GXT) using an **electrocardiogram** (ECG) to evaluate heart rate, blood pressure, ventilation, and oxygen uptake responses during exercise.

- **Step Tests:** A less-expensive testing method, step tests may be offered to healthy individuals who want to begin an aerobic exercise program.
  Step tests are designed to measure cardiovascular endurance and reveal how quickly the heart rate returns to normal after exercise. Step tests vary in style and intensity, and different tests are used around the world.
  A few examples include the YMCA Three-Minute Step Test, the Harvard Step Test, the Chester Step Test, the Canadian Home Fitness Test, the Queens College Step Test, and the Sharkey/Forestry Step Test.
  While techniques vary, in a typical test clients will step on an off a step or bench for a series of seconds or minutes, after which their pulses are checked to determine heart rate during and after exercise. Some tests (like the Balke) calculate energy expenditure; others refer to prepared charts that indicate recommended pulse rates for sex and age.

- **Bruce Protocol:** The most widely (and internationally) used protocol for graded exercise testing is the **Bruce Protocol**[3] (or treadmill) test, which is a great indicator of **functional capacity** (how much the heart works, and how much oxygen one consumes). To record heart rate, ECG leads are placed on the chest wall.

  - **Target Population**: Patients with suspected coronary heart disease; athletes who participate in sports with an emphasis on aerobic endurance; individuals who have mentioned experiencing chest pain, difficulty breathing, accelerated heart rate, etc.

  - **Advantages**: Provides a measurement of maximum heart rate, information which is essential to setting the intensity of exercise programs.

  - **Disadvantages**: Lengthy time requirements; large costs; requires a trained specialist to interpret ECG traces.

The test typically begins by running at an incline or gradient of 10%, speed 2.74 km/h. Every three minutes, the incline and speed of the treadmill will increase. Each level will see a 2% increase, as shown on the following chart:

Levels of the Bruce Protocol Test

Level	Incline	Speed	Speed	Gradient
1	10%	2.74 km/h	1.7 mph	10
2	12%	4.02 km/h	2.5 mph	12
3	14%	5.47 km/h	3.4 mph	14
4	16%	6.76 km/h	4.2 mph	16
5	18%	8.05 km/h	5.0 mph	18
6	20%	8.85 km/h	5.5 mph	20
7	22%	9.65 km/h	6.0 mph	22
8	24%	10.46 km/h	6.5 mph	24
9	26%	11.26 km/h	7.0 mph	26
10	28%	12.07 km/h	7.5 mph	28

The Bruce Protocol Treadmill test measures maximal fitness, and so the individual will run or walk until they tire, with the result looking at the maximum time spent running (in minutes).

- **Formula for Estimating VO2 Max (Maximal Oxygen Intake)**: Maximal Oxygen Intake (VO2 max) is a measure of cardiorespiratory fitness. It is a product of maximal cardiac output and arterial–venous oxygen difference. It is measured through an open circuit spirometer.
     Naturally, you may encounter patients who do not fit easily into each category. Do your best with a similar population, and choose which one best suits your needs.

---

[3] Have medical assistance, or test modifications, ready for those individuals with health problems, injuries, or low fitness levels.

T = Total time on the treadmill, measured as a fraction of a minute.
(i.e., A test time of 9 minutes and 30 seconds would be written as "T = 9.5.")

General:
$$VO2 \text{ max} = 14.76 - (1.379 * T) + (0.451 * T^2) - (0.012 * T^3).$$

For Women:
$$VO2 \text{ max} = 4.38 * T - 3.9.$$
- or -
$$VO2 \text{ max} = 2.94 * T + 3.74.$$

For Young Men:
$$VO2 \text{ max} = 2.94 * T - 3.9.$$

For Men:
$$VO2 \text{ max} = 2.94 * T + 7.65.$$

For those individuals that cannot walk or run on a treadmill, diagnostic testing through chemical tests is also an option. Persantine, Lexiscan TM, and dobutamine are some such chemical tests which allow for myocardial perfusion imaging.

Individuals with neuromuscular disorders who still require assessments for functional capacity and other such measurements can utilize the **cycle ergometer**, which is a low-impact machine. For those without leg performance, **arm ergometers** are another option.

Muscular Strength and Endurance
Muscular strength is the ability to exert maximal force during limited repetitions using maximum or near maximum resistance. In strength training, people usually focus on increasing muscle mass and power; improving muscular endurance is secondary. Generated force is specific to the muscles involved, as well as the type, speed, and joint angle of the contraction.

Isotonic Contraction: Contraction wherein the muscle remains unchanged, and the distance between the origin and insertion shortens.

Isometric: Muscle contraction without shortening or change in distance between the origin and insertion.

Eccentric vs. Concentric
When the muscle shortens to move the load, the isometric contraction is considered **concentric**; whereas muscles are **eccentric** when they are lengthening during contraction.
 For example, consider a bicep curl exercise. **Concentric**: On the upward curl, the brachialis and the biceps branch shorten, pulling up the forearm with the weight. **Eccentric**: Now, if the weight was too heavy and began to fall, then the brachialis and biceps muscles would still be contracting (trying to hold up the weight) while lengthening.

Isokinetic: Pertains to the concentric (shortening) muscle or eccentric (lengthening) muscle, in which the speed and tension are constant throughout the range of lengthening or contracting.

Muscular strength tests are typically expressed in terms of how much weight can be lifted.

1RM Testing

This test measures the heaviest weight which can be lifted under the maintenance of good form, and is considered the gold standard for evaluating dynamic strength. The following are the typical steps for 1RM testing:

1. Once the client is familiarized with the necessary movement, have her undergo a light warm-up of 5 – 10 reps at 40 – 60% (light-to-moderate exertion) of her perceived maximum resistance.

2. Instruct the client to first rest for 1 minute of light stretching, and then to perform 3 – 5 reps at 60 – 80% (moderate to heavy exertion) of perceived maximum resistance.

3. Add 5 – 10 pounds. If the client successfully lifts that weight, allow a rest period of 5 – 10 minutes before adding another 5 – 10 pounds. Repeat until client cannot lift the adjusted weight. Record the last successfully completed lift as the 1RM.

4. To express the results relative to the client's weight, divide the 1RM by her body weight.

Handgrip Dynamometer

Also called the "Grip Strength Test," this tracks the development of a client's grip strength. The following are the typical steps for Handgrip Testing:

1. Have the client grip the dynamometer with their dominant hand, and apply as much pressure as possible.

2. Record the maximum reading (kg).

3. Repeat three times, using the highest value to assess the client's performance based upon the normative data for the grip strength test.

Mean Handgrip Strength in Kilograms[4]

Age	Female		Male	
	Right Hand	Left Hand	Right Hand	Left Hand
20 – 29	30	28	47	45
30 – 39	31	29	47	47
40 – 49	29	28	47	45
50 – 59	28	26	45	43
60 – 69	24	23	40	38
70 +	20	19	33	32

Muscular endurance, on the other hand, is the exertion of sub-maximal force, or using less than maximum resistance, during repetitions of a movement. In improving endurance, people focus on improving the muscle's ability to work over time, rather than on gaining muscle mass and power. During muscular endurance testing, it is important to not allow any rest periods between repetitions.

---

[4] Massy-Westropp et al, "Hand Grip Strength: age and gender stratified normative data in a population-based study," *BMC Res Notes* 4, No. 127 (2011). Published online April 14, 2011, accessed October 9, 2015, http://www.ncbi.nlm.nih.gov/pmc/articles/PMC3101655/.

The American College of Sports Medicine's Partial Curl-Up Test

1. The client assumes the following position: supine on a mat, low back flat, knees bent at a ninety-degree angle, arms at the side with palms facing down, middle finger of each hand touching a piece of tape placed next to the body. A second piece of tape is placed ten centimeters beyond the first piece.

2. Set a metronome to the count of fifty bpm. (Metronomes encourage controlled movement; if one is unavailable, count off at the client's pace.) Have the client move through the range of motion, curling up to touch the second piece of tape before returning to the first in a controlled manner to the metronome's beat. The trunk ought to make a thirty-degree angle with the mat.

3. Client should perform as many curl-ups as possible without pause, up to a maximum of twenty-five, for one minute.

The American College of Sports Medicine's Push-Up Test

1. Starting position:
   - For Males: Standard "down" push-up position, with the toes as the pivotal point: hands shoulder-width apart, back straight, head up.

   - For Females: Modified "knee" push-up position: hands shoulder-width apart, back straight, lower legs together and in contact with the mat, ankles plantar flexed, head up.

2. Have the client raise his body by straightening his arms, before returning to the starting position to touch his chin to the mat. The stomach should never touch the mat. (Both males and females should keep their backs straight at all times. Push-up must be to a straight-arm position.)

3. Count the maximal number of push-ups performed in good form. Stop when the client cannot maintain good form on two consecutive reps, or strains forcibly and cannot continue.

Body Composition

Bodies are made up of varying amounts of water, proteins, minerals, and fat. Assessing body composition can determine the amount of fat, bone and muscle in an individual's body. In the human body, muscle tissue takes up less space than fat tissue, but weighs significantly more. Therefore, body composition and weight combined determine the leanness and fitness of an individual.

BMI

A client's height and weight makes up their **body mass index**.

$$BMI = 703 * \frac{Weight\ (lbs)}{Height\ (in)^2}$$

Underweight	< 18
Normal Weight	18.5 – 24.9
Overweight	25 – 29.9
Obese	≥ 30

A BMI reading is not completely accurate as it does not consider factors such as body frame, age, or percentage of fat. Therefore, a patient's **body composition** (percent body fat) is often a more reliable way to classify body weight.

Skinfolds

This method measures an individual's subcutaneous fat thickness with a caliper at certain points in the body. Ensure that the skin is dry; do not take measurements after physical exertion to ensure that the skin is free from bodily fluids. There should be no oils or lotions on the skin. Measurements should be taken on the *right* side of the body.

1. Identify and mark measurable skinfold sites.

2. Following the natural cleavage lines of the skin, and using the thumb and index finger (holding them perpendicular to the skinfold and about three inches apart), grasp the skinfold firmly about a half inch above the site to be measured. (Do not release your grip while measuring.)

3. Place the jaws of the caliper approximately one-half inch (one centimeter) below the thumb and index finger; always release the caliper jaw pressure slowly

4. Four seconds after the pressure is released, take the skinfold measurement. Measure to the nearest one-half to one millimeter.

Take at least two measurements at each site. Proceed in a rotation rather than by taking consecutive readings at the same site. Take additional measurements if the values differ by more than one millimeter.

Measuring Sites for Women

Triceps: Keeping the elbow extended and the arm relaxed, measure a vertical fold of skin at the posterior midline of the upper arm midway between the top of the shoulder and the elbow joint.

Thigh: Measure a vertical fold on the front of the thigh halfway between the knee and the hip.

Suprailium: Imagine a line extending from the anterior of the armpit (the anterior axillary line) to the hipbone. Measure a diagonal fold above the crest of the hip bone, or ilium, along this imaginary line.

Measuring Sites for Men

Chest: Measure a diagonal fold halfway between the anterior of the armpit (the anterior axillary line) and nipple.

Abdomen: Measure a vertical fold of skin about two centimeters laterally to the right of the umbilicus (belly button).

Thigh: Measure a vertical fold on the front of the thigh halfway between the knee and the hip.

Bioelectrical Impedance Analysis

The most prevalent component of the human body is water, which makes up approximately fifty-five to seventy-eight percent of a human body. Since water conducts electricity, Bioelectrical Impedance Analysis (BIA) measures body composition through the administration of a safe, low-level current that flows through these intracellular and extracellular bodily fluids.

The BIA technique calculates an individual's total body water; the fat-free weight can then be extrapolated from that number. Electrodes are attacked to a patient's hands and feet while the patient is lying down. This method of body composition analysis, although more lengthy and expensive, is believed to be more accurate than skinfold measurements.

Implications of Assessment

The minimum recommended level of total body fat for men is five percent and for women is fifteen percent The ranges for optimal health are ten to twenty-five percent body fat for men and eighteen to thirty percent body fat for women. These percentages and ranges tend to be lower for athletes in order to enhance body productivity and performance.

Flexibility

A client's **flexibility** is his or her possible range of motion around a specific joint or series of articulations. The ability to move a joint through an adequate range of movement is important for daily activities, as well as sports performance. Without normal movement within a joint, a person may not be able to function normally. While lack of flexibility may not seem like a very severe problem, a constant tightness in the muscles due to not stretching can lead to muscle pain, stiffness, and even injury. Assessments help determine a person's risk for future pain and injury.

Sit and Reach Test

This is the most common way to measure lower back, hamstring length, and hip joint flexibility. However, it does not effectively measure the lower back's range of motion (ROM).

- **Equipment required:** Sit and reach box (or, a ruler used along with a step or box)

- **Procedure:** Have the client remove his shoes and sit on the floor with his legs stretched out straight ahead. The client should press the soles of his feet firmly against the box; locking the knees, press the legs flat against the floor. If the client requires assistance, hold his legs down.
    Have the client reach forward as far as possible along the measuring line, keeping palms facing downwards, hands side by side or one on top of the other, and in alignment. Have the client reach out and hold the position for one or two seconds and record the distance. Ensure that the movements are smooth, without jerking or thrusting.

- **Scoring:** Record the client's score to the nearest centimeter or half inch that he were able to reach with his hand. The zero mark is located at the level of the feet on some tests; other tests set the zero mark nine inches before the feet. One modified sit and reach test adjusts the zero mark according to the subject's arm and leg length. The following table provides a general guide for expected scores (in centimeters and inches) for adults, using zero at the level of the feet (otherwise, add twenty-three centimeters or nine inches).

ACSM Sit and Reach Test Scores

Percentile Rank	Men		Women	
	20 – 29 years	30 – 39 years	20 – 29 years	30 – 39 years
	inches	inches	inches	inches
99	>23.0	>22.0	>24.0	>24.0
90	21.75	21.0	23.75	22.5
80	20.5	19.5	22.5	21.5
70	19.5	18.5	21.5	20.5
60	18.5	17.5	20.5	20.0
50	17.5	16.5	20.0	19.0
40	16.5	15.5	19.25	18.25
30	15.5	14.5	18.25	17.25
20	14.5	13.0	17.0	16.5
10	12.25	11.0	15.5	14.5
01	<10.5	<9.25	<14.0	<12.0

A fitness assessment may also utilize physical and laboratory tests.

Resting heart rate
Resting heart rate (HR) is obtained at the **apical site** (over the heart, at the fifth intercostal) with a stethoscope. Palpitation of the apical pulse is the point of maximal pulse (**PMI**). A normal resting HR is sixty to eighty beats per minute.

Resting blood pressure
Resting blood pressure (BP) can be taken when the patient is seated, supine, or standing. BP is notated as the maximal output (the **systolic** reading) over the minimum output (**diastolic**). This notation is not a fraction, and cannot be reduced.

- **Normal BP**: Less than 120/80.

- **Pre-hypertensive**: 120-139/80-89.

- **Stage 1 hypertension (HTN)**: 140-159/90-99.

- **Stage 2 HTN**: Greater than 160/100.

Goals

Setting goals for each client is essential when creating a comprehensive exercise program that builds strength and balance while improving cardiovascular function. To accomplish these goals, you must apply your knowledge of exercise physiology, safety concerns, and the client's own limitations (i.e. past injuries, surgeries, age, likes and dislikes for a particular exercise, etc.). You must also realize the necessity of fine-tuning goals as progress is made: keep track of measurements, changes in physique/capabilities, etc.

Remember: The easiest way of ascertaining clients' progress is also the most important way—talk to them! How are they feeling; do they have more energy or strength; are they sleeping better; do they feel any pain in the body? Communication is key to establishing mutually-agreed upon goals and means.

For example, a client may say that she has zero interest in machine training—she prefers using free weights only. You would therefore do your best to design a program using only free weights while considering muscular strength/endurance, body composition, cardiovascular health, and flexibility. Of course, customized programs using kettle bells, exercise bands, hand weights, and core work are plentiful—the most important thing is to make sure that you and your client are on the same page.

There are two types of goals, which you may have also learned as "objectives," that you will encounter both on the test and throughout your career.

Outcome Goals: As the name suggests, these goals refer to the desired end result of the program: weight loss, increased flexibility, improvements with muscular strength, etc. One of the most popular occurrences comes with the New Year: "This year, I'm going to lose weight!"

While highly motivating, these goals are long-term and lack a specific process.

Process Goals: These can be used to establish a plan for achieving an outcome goal, or they can simply apply to independent situations. Process goals deal with the strategy necessary to high performance: sort of a one-step-at-a-time goal process.

Perhaps your client wants to complete ten reps with a heavier free weight. Those ten reps are readily attainable, and so this is a process goal. Careful though! It's possible that this client has never successfully completed ten reps with free weights, making this an outcome goal. It's important to learn the client's limitations and experience before creating their program.

Discuss short-term and long-term goals with your clients that will help motivate and educate them for best results. Adding exercises as they continue to improve and gain strength will help them understand the importance of exercise as a lifetime commitment. Setting goals with a client involves putting safety first in training each muscle group in a slow and controlled manner. Obviously, there are exceptions to this if your client is training for a competitive sport. These exercise programs need to be balanced; prevent injuries through strengthening those areas that have muscular imbalances.

How to Communicate both Improvements and Regressions over Time
A personal trainer needs to evaluate the progress made with a client based on the progress made from the initial fitness assessments to the present moment, usually every three to four weeks. Input should be provided as to the progress made through improvements in measurements, increased strength and weight loss. It is an ongoing process where communication between the trainer and the client is very important for best results.

The First Month
Most clients will feel the difference after the first month of training on a consistent basis, with visible results after sixty days. Family, friends and co-workers will really start to see the difference in the person being trained. During the first month of training, muscular strength and endurance as well as improvements in cardiovascular endurance improve rapidly. It is always amazing to see

how quickly the body adapts to exercise, especially if it has not been part of a regular habit. Flexibility is the one area that does take time and patience is key.

The Second Month
Improvements will continue to show in muscle strength and endurance (including cardiovascular); however it is important as a trainer to adjust a client's program to avoid any plateaus to ensure continued progress in all areas. The second month is when body composition begins to improve, especially if proper nutrition is being followed. Stretching and flexibility will slowly improve and should continue to be a part of the exercise program and training.

The Third Month
Body composition continues to improve, and this phase of training will show significant improvements as the client is now considered to be in a trained state. Improving the results of muscular strength and endurance will gradually become more difficult; however improvement in flexibility will be noticeable. The trainer as well as the client will see an increased range of motion with less tension in the muscles. Persistence pays off in the long run.

Domain II: Program Design and Implementation

Before you can begin to correctly prescribe exercise in any form, it's important for you yourself to understand the kinesiology, biomechanics, anatomy, etc. of the human body.

Exercise Science covers a broad range of topics: physical activity, exercise, athletic performance, etc. Understanding how the body works is essential to providing safe and effective exercise prescriptions.

BIOENERGETICS

All movement within our body—in fact, every operation in our body—depends upon energy to function. **Bioenergetics** describes the processes of transferring energy from consumed foods throughout the body, supplying the contracting muscles with usable energy called adenosine triphosphate **(ATP).** This energy, or fuel, drives the body to operate.

ATP is necessary for all energy-requiring processes in cells. All muscle cells contain a small amount of ATP at all times, but that ATP is consumed almost immediately after exercise starts.

To replenish this energy, and maintain activity, ATP must be replenished via other energy pathways or energy systems.

Systems

There are three systems to know when covering bioenergetics:

1. **The Phosphagen System** is the body's energy system that uses immediate stored energy inside the muscle cell. This energy system is composed of ATP and phosphocreatine (PCr). Phosphocreatine and ATP are stored inside the muscles cells. Phosphocreatine is used for all-out effort and explosive power exercises like **sprinting** and **weightlifting**. The phosphocreatine system can sustain physical activity for no more than thirty seconds.

2. **The Nonoxidative System**, sometimes called the lactic acid or glycolytic system, is the body's short-term energy system. It allows ATP and phosphocreatine to be resynthesized at a rapid rate.
   This system is sometimes referred to as the **anaerobic** (without oxygen) pathway, because oxygen is not required for ATP production. Instead, this system uses carbohydrates (glucose and glycogen) for ATP production.
   The nonoxidative system is sometimes referred to as the **lactic acid system**, because lactic acid is produced when carbohydrates are broken down without the use of oxygen. Lactic acid, or lactate, accumulates in the muscles and contributes to muscle fatigue.
   The nonoxidative system is used for physical activities that require high-intensity effort. It provides energy to the working muscles during activities which last from thirty seconds to three minutes. These activities can be anything from running up the stairs to passing another participant in a race.

3. **The Oxidative System** is the body's long-term energy system. It breaks down carbohydrates (glucose and glycogen) *and* fats (lipids) from the foods in order to synthesize ATP. In this energy

system, a very limited extent of proteins can be broken down into glucose as well, but proteins are not a preferred fuel source.

       This system is also called the **aerobic** (with oxygen) pathway, because oxygen is required for this system to proceed. This system produces a large amount of ATP, unlike the phosphagen system and the nonoxidative system. The oxidative system's metabolic by-products are water and carbon dioxide. (Remember, the nonoxidative system's by-product: lactic acid.) Unlike lactic acid, water and carbon dioxide do not cause the muscle to fatigue.

       The oxidative system produces energy for those physical activities that last more than three minutes; as well as those activities where intensity is limited, like running a marathon or hiking. While this system produces a larger amount of ATP than the other systems, it takes a longer time to produce that energy. Therefore, when the working muscle demands more than is being provided, the muscle will rely on the nonoxidative system for energy as well. This cooperation between the oxidative and nonoxidative systems is called the **anaerobic or lactate threshold**.

Metabolic Processes and Energy Production

The process of creating energy in the human body is called cellular respiration and occurs mostly within the mitochondria, or "power house" of the cell. Humans derive our energy from ATP (Adenosine Triphosphate) which is created by breaking down glucose (which you may recall, comes from carbohydrates). The three major phases of cellular respiration are Glycolysis, the Krebs Cycle, and the Electron Transport Chain.

The following pages provide a breakdown of the three pathways listed above. There's no need for you to memorize the chemistry of the processes—indeed, we hardly cover that here. You do, however, need to have a basic understanding of the differences between the three, and the functions which they perform.

1. **Glycolysis**: The process of converting glucose into pyruvate releases free energy, which in turn is used to form ATP and NADH. Glycolysis can occur without the presence of oxygen, and takes place within the cytoplasm of the cell.

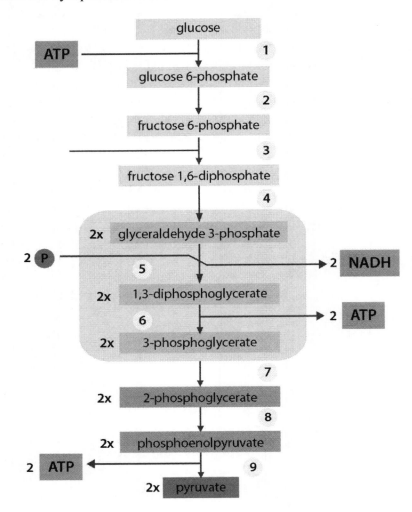

Glycolysis therefore produces four ATP and two NADH per glucose. The pyruvate created by this process is used during the Krebs Cycle to create even more ATP.

2. **Krebs Cycle:** Unlike glycolysis, the Krebs Cycle does require oxygen to create ATP—this classifies it as a form of **aerobic respiration**. Aerobic respiration produces more energy than glycolysis, and can be broken down into two parts: the Krebs Cycle and the Electron Transport Chain. The Krebs Cycle is also known as the Citric Acid Cycle.

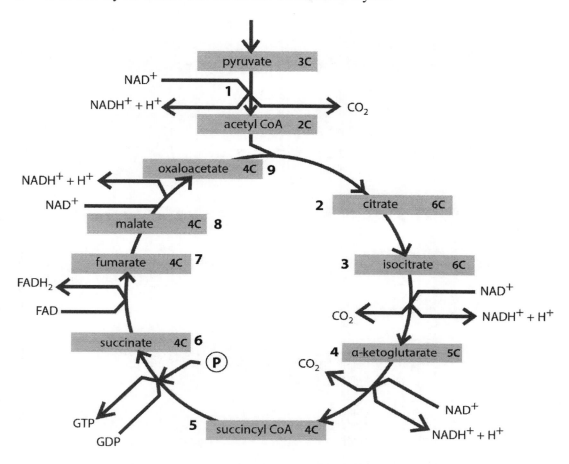

You may be wondering why the Cycle repeats. Glycolysis produces two pyruvate molecules from each glucose; each glucose thus undergoes the Krebs Cycle twice. During the Krebs Cycle, six NADH2, two FADH2, and two ATP are produced per glucose.

3. **Electron Transport Chain:** The NADH and the FADH produced by the Krebs Cycle have received high energy electrons from the pyruvic acid that was broken down in the Krebs Cycle. Therefore, the NADH and FADH work as carrier molecules, able to transport the energy created by the Krebs Cycle and Glycolysis to the Electron Transport Chain (located in the inner mitochondrial membrane).

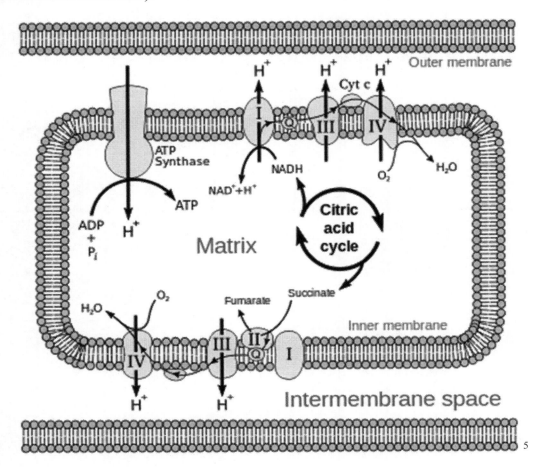

When glucose is ingested, it goes through these metabolic pathways, reacting with substrates in different parts of the body in order to eventually create ATP. One glucose molecule can create between thirty to thirty-two ATP. However, we use hundreds of thousands of ATP every day; therefore this process is essential and occurs quickly. The reason that humans need to breathe is to enable the aerobic process of creating ATP, so that we can have energy to complete basic tasks and live. ATP production through cellular respiration in the mitochondria is essential for life.

---

[5] "Mitochondrial electron transport chain—Etc4" by Fvasconcellos 22:35, 9 September 2007 (UTC) - Vector version of w:Image:Etc4.png by TimVickers, content unchanged.. Licensed under Public Domain via Commons - https://commons.wikimedia.org/wiki/File:Mitochondrial_electron_transport_chain%E2%80%94Etc4.svg#/media/File:Mitochondrial_electron_transport_chain%E2%80%94Etc4.svg

Female Athlete Triad
Female Athlete Triad describes a trio of serious health problems that commonly occur in female athletes: eating disorders or disordered eating, low bone mass, and amenorrhea (when the menstrual cycle stops). Society reinforces unhealthy and unrealistic expectations for female (and male) body types, but sports that emphasize being thin (such as cross country running, dancing, etc.) are more likely to produce athletes with these conditions.

The following is a list of risk factors associated with this disorder:

- Participation in sports or physical activities that require a certain weight or that require weight checks.

- Social isolation due to athletic activities.

- Excessive exercise or training.

- Overwhelming pressure to attain victory or success in sports or athletic activities.

- Negative consequences for weight gain.

- Negative influence from overbearing parents and/or coaches

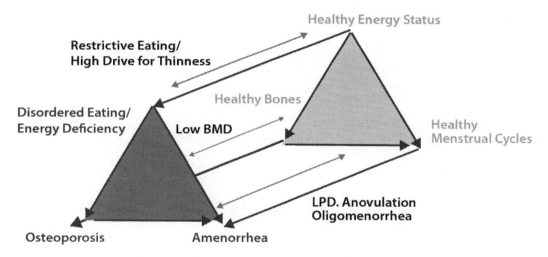

Chronic energy deficiency is a primary cause of those health problems related to the Female Athlete Triad. Because of either intentional caloric restriction or excessive exercise, athletes with the disorder do not consume enough calories to compensate for the energy expenditure resulting from daily exercise and training.

A comprehensive approach to preventing Female Athlete Triad should not only focus on education about nutrition and clinical eating disorders like anorexia nervosa and bulimia nervosa, but also consider subclinical disordered eating behaviors like caloric restriction. Not all athletes meet the criteria for an eating disorder, but they may fall into this subclinical category, be overly concerned with body weight and body image, and therefore risk being affected by Female Athlete Triad.

Blood

Blood has many functions, but its most important job is the transport of oxygen to working muscles, tissues, and organs.

Plasma

Plasma is the fluid part of the blood. Its main component is water (comprising ninety to ninety-three percent of the plasma) but it also contains some proteins, electrolytes, gases, nutrients, waste products, and various hormones.

While plasma carries a small amount of oxygen, most of the body's oxygen is delivered through the cells of the blood.

Erythrocytes are red blood cells, and they contain a protein called **hemoglobin**. These are the most abundant types of cells in blood, accounting for more than ninety-nine percent of the blood's cells. Oxygen is bound to hemoglobin for transportation; hemoglobin also carries about thirty percent of the carbon dioxide in the body.

> A **hematocrit** is a blood test that measures the amount of erythrocytes within the blood. The hematocrit levels are slightly higher in men than in woman, due to higher testosterone levels.

Leukocytes are white blood cells. They are the body's defense system, working to destroy any potentially infectious agents that enter the body.

Platelets are made up of many other parts of cells. They go wherever there is damage to the wall of a blood vessel to stop blood loss. If a body part is cut, platelets rush to the scene to clot the blood so that a person would not bleed out.

The Effects of Exercise on Blood

Hyperemia is the increased amount of blood flow to the working muscles of the body. As exercise increases, so too does the delivery of oxygen and nutrients to the muscles. This in turn increases the removal of waste products such as lactate and carbon dioxide.

Cardiovascular drift occurs when prolonged endurance exercise increases body temperature. To prevent overheating, plasma is moved from the blood vessels into the surrounding tissue. This provides the body with more water for sweating, which cools down the body. This drift can cause increased heart rate, because it decreases the total volume of blood and decreases the stroke volume.

In turn, the movement of plasma out of the blood leads to **hemoconcentration**—a decrease of fluids within the blood—which makes sense, since plasma is the fluid part of the blood. Hemoconcentration can lead to elevations in hematocrit and hemoglobin values.

Endurance training produces more erythrocytes (red blood cells), and therefore more hemoglobin, which increases the oxygen carrying capacity of blood to the working muscles. Training also prompts an increased plasma volume, which leads to a higher stroke volume and lower resting heart rate.

Anatomy and Physiology of Cardiovascular and Pulmonary Systems

The **pulmonary system** is divided into the upper and lower respiratory tracks.

- The upper respiratory track consists of the nose, the pharynx (throat), and larynx (voice box).

- The lower respiratory track consists of the trachea (wind pipe), lungs, bronchi, bronchioles (passage ways into the alveoli), and the alveoli (air sacs).

The human body has two lungs; these are organs that help us breath in air. The right lung has three lobes, and the left lung has two lobes. The lungs occupy pleural cavities that are covered by a **pleural membrane**. The pleural membrane helps separate the two lungs from each other.

The **apex**, the top of each lung, extends into the base of the neck above the first rib. Each lung has a **base** as well, which rests on the diaphragm.

The **diaphragm** is a respiratory muscle that allows us to breathe. It is dome-shaped, and it separates the abdominal cavity (stomach) from the thoracic cavity (chest). This muscle contracts and relaxes as we breathe.

As we breathe through our nose and mouth, air passes through the pharynx and larynx and down through the cartilage-lined trachea into our lungs. Air then passes through the bronchiole tubes into a cluster of **alveoli**. Alveoli are air sacs that exchange gases (oxygen and carbon dioxide) between our lungs and the blood.

Inhalation causes the diaphragm to move downward; the intercostal muscles (muscles between the ribs) then pull the ribcage up, enlarging the thoracic (chest) cavity.

Exhalation causes the diaphragm to move upward. Now the intercostal muscles relax, causing less pressure inside the thoracic cavity. However, there is an increased pressure inside the lungs, which causes air to be expelled through the nose and mouth.

Trachea

Another name for the trachea is the wind pipe. It is made up of C-shaped cartilage rings that serve three important functions:

1. The C-shaped cartilage rings offer support for the trachea. They support, protect, and maintain an open airway.

2. The tough cartilage prevents overexpansion of the respiratory system.

3. The trachea lies anterior to the esophagus; it supports the esophagus, and allows for large amounts of food to pass down into the stomach by collapsing slightly.

Assessing the carotid and radial pulses

Heart rate, called a **pulse** due to the pulsating feeling in the blood vessels near the skin, can be measured on any large or medium-sized artery. Gentle compression of the artery by the index and middle finger together allows for the detection of a pulse. The two most common arteries that are assessed are the carotid artery (in the neck) and the radial artery (in the wrist).

The **carotid artery** is divided into the left and right carotid, and lies on each side of the neck. It runs along the side of the trachea (windpipe) and below the mandible (jaw bone).

To assess the carotid pulse, place index and middle finger below the jaw and the side of the neck. Hold fingers together and press gently; move fingers around until pulse is felt.

Count the number of times the pulse is felt in 10 seconds using a second hand watch. Multiply this number by six to find the amount of heart beats in one minute.

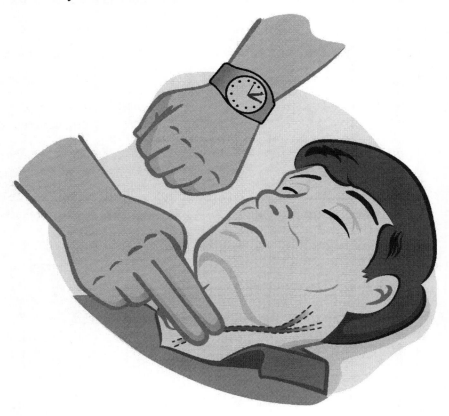

The **radial artery** branches off the brachial artery (major blood vessel of the upper arm) and runs towards the thumb along the forearm.

To assess pulse, place index and middle finger together and press gently on the thumb side of the wrist until pulse is felt. If no pulse is felt, move fingers around until pulse is felt.

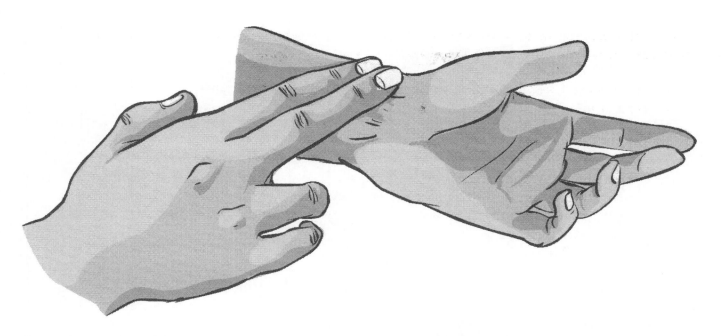

Count the number of times the pulse is felt in 10 seconds, and multiply that by six to find the amount of heart beats in one minute.

The **Cardiovascular System** consists of the heart, as well as two networks of blood vessels called the **pulmonary** and **systemic** circulatory systems.

1. **Pulmonary Circulation**: The part of the cardiovascular system that works with the lungs. The right atrium in the heart receives oxygen-depleted blood from the body. The heart then pumps oxygen-depleted blood into the lungs to be re-oxygenated. The left atrium receives that oxygenated blood from the lungs.

2. **Systemic Circulation**: The part of the cardiovascular system that circulates blood to all parts of the body, except for the lungs. It transports oxygenated blood away from the heart and carries oxygen-depleted blood back towards the heart.

Anatomy of the Heart

The heart is a very complex system made up of four chambers, four valves, and multiple blood vessels.

The **four chambers** are the right atria, the left atria, the right ventricle, and the left ventricle.

Inside the ventricles are the four valves:

1. **Tricuspid Valve**: Located between the right atrium and the right ventricle.

2. **Bicuspid (mitral) Valve**: Located between the left atrium and left ventricle.

3. **Pulmonic Valve**: Located between the right ventricle and pulmonary artery.

4. **Aortic Valve**: Located between the left ventricle and the aorta.

Valves regulate the pressure inside the ventricles and prevent backflow. As blood fills the ventricles, the valves start to close; this builds up pressure. When the pressure is very high, the ventricle will contract and squeeze out the blood forcefully, either into the lungs or out of the aorta to the rest of the body.

The heart is connected to the rest of the body through a series of blood vessels. These are: **arteries**, **arterioles**, **capillaries**, **venules**, and **veins**.

Arteries are large blood vessels. They carry oxygenated blood away from the heart. To remember this, associate the "a" in "artery" with "away." (**A**rteries carry blood **a**way from the heart.)

Arteries branch into smaller arteries called **arterioles**, which in turn branch off to form **capillaries**. Capillaries are extremely small, and they allow for the exchange of nutrients and gases within the tissue.

As these exchanges take place, several capillaries will join to form **venules**. Venules return oxygen-depleted blood back towards heart.

Just as the larger arteries grew smaller the further away from the heart they went, so too do the venules grow larger as they return to the heart. A number of venules form the larger blood vessels called **veins**. Veins create more pressure inside the blood vessel, which helps return oxygen-depleted blood back to the heart.

The following chart illustrates the flow of blood through the heart.

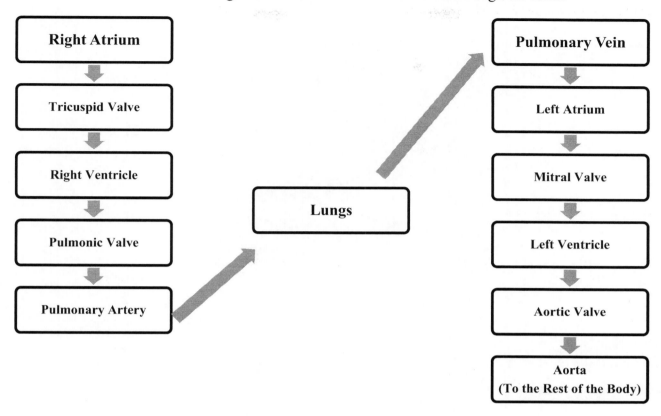

Oxygen-depleted blood is returned to the heart through the **inferior vena cava** (the large vein that carries oxygen-depleted blood into the heart from the lower half of the body) or the **superior vena cava** (the large vein that carries oxygen-depleted blood from the upper half of the body).

Blood enters the right atrium. The blood flows through the tricuspid valve into the right ventricle.

After the blood finishes filling the right ventricle, the tricuspid valve closes to allow pressure build up and to prevent blood from flowing back into the right atrium.

The right ventricle will then forcefully squeeze the blood through the pulmonic valve into the pulmonary artery; the pulmonary artery takes the blood away from the heart and into the lungs.

Inside the lungs, gases are exchanged. Oxygenated blood is picked up and returned to the heart via the pulmonary vein. From the pulmonary vein, blood enters the left atrium and then flows through the mitral valve (also called the bicuspid valve) into the left ventricle.

After the left ventricle is filled, the mitral valve closes to allow pressure build up and to prevent blood from flowing back into the left atrium.

Pressure builds up due to the closed bicuspid (mitral) valve, and, after enough pressure is built up inside the left ventricle, oxygenated blood will be forcefully expelled through the aortic valve into the aorta. The aortic valve prevents blood from flowing back into the left ventricle. Oxygenated blood will then be distributed throughout the body. The left ventricle will pump oxygenated blood out through the **aorta** (the largest artery in the body) that will be distributed to all organs and tissue throughout the body.

The right and left sides of the heart are separated by the septum. When the ventricles are pumping, the atria are relaxing, and vice versa.

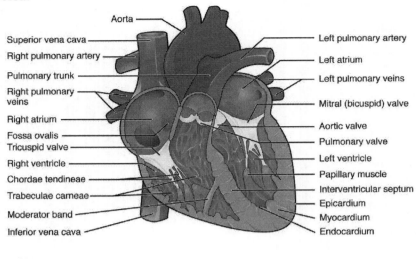

Aorta
Superior vena cava
Right pulmonary artery
Pulmonary trunk
Right pulmonary veins
Right atrium
Fossa ovalis
Tricuspid valve
Right ventricle
Chordae tendineae
Trabeculae carneae
Moderator band
Inferior vena cava

Left pulmonary artery
Left atrium
Left pulmonary veins
Mitral (bicuspid) valve
Aortic valve
Pulmonary valve
Left ventricle
Papillary muscle
Interventricular septum
Epicardium
Myocardium
Endocardium

Anterior view [6]

The Cardiac Cycle

The **cardiac cycle** makes up the pumping action of the heart, and is the sequence of events which lead up to the contraction of the heart.

The contraction of the heart muscle (the myocardium) is called **systole.** When the heart muscle relaxes, it is called **diastole.** Remember the two numbers used in the measurement of blood pressure? The systolic, or top number, represents when the heart is contracting. The diastolic, or bottom number, represents the relaxing of the heart.

Stroke volume (SV) is the volume of blood being ejected from the left ventricle on every contraction. The stroke volume at rest is usually **70 ml.**

Heart rate (HR) is the number of times a heart beats per minute. When the body is at rest, heart rate can be about **72 beats per minute**.

Cardiac output (Q) is the amount of blood that is ejected from the left ventricle every minute. Heart rate and stroke volume produces cardiac output: **Q = HR * SV**

Cardiac output at rest is usually about **5 L per minute**.

HR (72 beats per minute) * SV (70 ml) = Q (5 L of blood per minute)

End-diastolic volume (EDV) is the amount of blood left in each ventricle after the heart muscle relaxes (diastole) during the cardiac cycle.

[6] "2008 Internal Anatomy of the HeartN" by OpenStax College - Anatomy & Physiology, Connexions Web site. http://cnx.org/content/col11496/1.6/, Jun 19, 2013. Licensed under CC BY 3.0 via Wikimedia Commons - https://commons.wikimedia.org/wiki/File:2008_Internal_Anatomy_of_the_HeartN.jpg#/media/File:2008_Internal_Anatomy_of_the_Heart N.jpg

End-systolic volume (ESV) is the amount of blood left in each ventricle after the heart contracts. ESV at rest equals about 55 ml of blood.

Ejection fraction (EF) is the percentage of blood in the ventricle when the heart is in a relaxation (diastolic) state; but this blood actually gets pumped out during the contraction (systolic) phase.

The Frank-Starling Law states that the amount of blood left in each ventricle after the heart muscle relaxes (EDV) will significantly affect the SV; this is because a large amount of blood left in each ventricle after every contraction creates a greater stretch on the heart muscle. Over time, as the ventricle stretch increases, contractile force increases. A normal EDV would be around 125 ml.

Effect of Exercise on Pulmonary and Cardiac Function

Pulmonary Function
Minute ventilation (VE) is the volume of air inhaled or exhaled in one minute. **At rest, minute ventilation is about 6 L/min.** Exercise increases **minute ventilation**, because breathing depth increases during physical activity.

Exercise also increases **respiratory rate**, evidenced by the increased number of breaths required as activity grows more intense. During maximal intensity exercise, minute ventilation may be twenty to twenty-five times higher than the typical 6 L/min that is seen at rest. This increase also causes **tidal volume** to increase.

Tidal volume is the amount of air entering or leaving the lungs in a single breath. The air that enters and leaves the lungs in a single breath is usually around **0.5 L to 4 L.**
Respiratory rate is the amount of breaths taken in one minute. Respiratory rate ranges from twelve breaths per minute to almost fifty breaths per minute, depending on exercise intensity.

In individuals who are healthy and who exercise regularly, exercise capacity is not limited by ventilation. Ventilatory capacity does not undergo any changes with long term exercise in healthy individuals.

Cardiac Function
Two major modifications during exercise work to increase oxygen delivery to the working muscle tissue. They are shunting and vasodilation.

1. **Shunting** is a term used when blood is shunted away from all the vital (visceral) organs of the body to the exercising muscles. As exercise increases, **vasoconstriction** (narrowing of the blood vessels) takes place in the arterioles within the visceral organs; at the same time, **vasodilation** (widening of the blood vessels) takes place in the blood vessels (arterioles) in the muscle. This shunting causes more blood delivery (and therefore **increased oxygen**) to the working muscles, and takes blood and oxygen away from the visceral organs.

2. As aerobic exercise increases, so too will the vasodilation of the blood vessels in the working muscle. **Vasodilation** causes the total peripheral resistance (resistance of blood vessels to the flow of blood) to decrease. This accommodates the rise in cardiac output that occurs during exercise.

The Skeletal System

The skeletal system is composed of all the bones of the body, and can be divided into the **axial skeleton** and the **appendicular skeleton**.

The skeletal system supports the body, protects the internal organs, and facilitates muscular movement.

Axial Skeleton
This skeleton includes all of the bones of the skull, vertebral column, ribs, and sternum. It supports and protects all of the internal organs.

Spine
The spine, or the vertebral column, provides the support of the skeletal structure. The human spine contains thirty-three vertebrae: seven cervical, twelve thoracic, five lumbar, five sacral, and four coccygeal (these bones are fused together to form one bone: the coccyx) vertebrae. Between each vertebra are intervertebral disks. These disks are flat and round, and are composed of fibrocartilaginous tissue.

Fibrocartilaginous Tissue
This tissue is strong and tough, but it allows for slight movement. Fibrocartilaginous tissue is composed of the annulus fibrosus, which is the outer portion of the disk. The nucleus pulposus is a jelly-like substance in the middle of each disk that allows the vertebrae to absorb shock and bear weight.

A commonly-found abnormal curvature of the spine is **scoliosis**, a lateral or sideways deviation of the spine. It is an abnormal curve of the spine in the frontal plane.
Kyphosis is an excessive outward curvature of the spine that causes a hunching of the back. These curves occur in the **thoracic and sacral regions**, and develop in the fetus.

Lordosis curvature, on the other hand, is an inward curvature of the spine. These curves occur in the **cervical and lumbar** regions, developing after birth.

The human body has twenty-four ribs: twelve ribs on each side of the spine. There are seven pairs of true ribs that attach to the sternum and spine; and five pairs of ribs do not attach to the sternum. The eighth, ninth, and tenth pairs of ribs are connected to the ribs above them, and the eleventh and twelfth pairs of ribs are called **floating ribs** (because their ends do not attach to anything).

The **sternum**, also called the breast bone, lies in the middle of the chest. It has three parts: the manubrium (superior), the body (middle), and the xiphoid process (inferior). The connection between the sternum and the ribs forms the ribcage, which serves as protection for the heart and lungs.

The Appendicular Skeleton
The other skeleton, the appendicular, consists of all the bones making up the arms, legs, pelvis, and pelvic girdle. This skeletal structure provides both movement and support.

The scapula and clavicles attach the limbs to the trunk of the body. The bones in the arms include the humerus, ulna, and radial bones. The glenoid fossa of the scapula attaches to the humerus, which in turn attaches to the ulna and radial bones that make up the forearm.

The pelvis and pelvic girdle connect the axial and appendicular skeletons. The pelvic girdle consists of the hip bones (ilium, ischium, and pubis), the sacrum, and the coccyx. The femur (the largest bone in the body), the tibia, and the fibula form the leg.

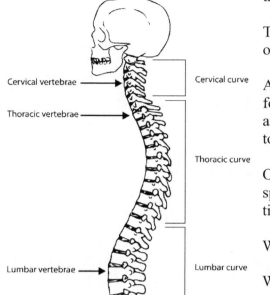

The bones of the spinal column are in specific order from the top of the spine to the end.

At the top of the spinal column are seven cervical vertebra, followed by twelve thoracic vertebra, then five lumbar, five sacral, and four coccygeal vertebrae. (The coccygeal vertebrae are fused together to form one bone: the coccyx.)

One way to remember how many true vertebra bones are in the spinal column is to correlate their numbers with typical meal times:

We eat breakfast at 7:00 am. (7 cervical)

We eat lunch at 12:00 noon. (12 thoracic)

We eat dinner at 5:00 pm. (5 lumbar) [7]

Muscles

There are three types of muscles:

1. Skeletal.

2. Cardiac.

3. Smooth. (Found in many parts of the body, including the blood vessels, the gastrointestinal tract, the bladder, and the uterus.)

Muscle Tissues
There are three different types of muscle tissue.

1. **Skeletal Muscle** is the most abundant tissue found in the human body, accounting for fifty percent of the body's mass. Skeletal muscle's primary job is to provide muscular contraction and relaxation to enable movement, whether someone is getting out of bed or bench pressing 150lbs. When you think of skeletal muscle, think of the body's skeletal structure: these are the muscles that attach to it.

---

[7] "Illu vertebral column" by . - http://training.seer.cancer.gov/module_anatomy/unit3_5_skeleton_divisions.html. Licensed under Public Domain via Wikimedia Commons -
https://commons.wikimedia.org/wiki/File:Illu_vertebral_column.jpg#/media/File:Illu_vertebral_column.jpg

2. **Striated muscle** is also another term for skeletal muscle because of the striations visible when looking at this muscle under a microscope; long and thin multinucleated fibers appear that are crossed with a regular pattern of fine red and white lines.

3. **Tendons** are what attach skeletal muscle to bones. If you think of bones as levers, the skeletal muscle is attached to the bones by tendons that provide the body with movement and mobility.

Skeletal Muscle

Skeletal Muscle is made up of many cells, called myofibers or myocytes. These cells are constructed and arranged to give the muscle its function. Skeletal muscle is orchestrated in a very fine fashion, consisting of the tendon attaching the muscle to the bone, all the way down to the myofibers.

The muscle is covered by a connective tissue called the **epimysium**, which surrounds the entire muscle. Each muscle contains a bundle or fascicle that is surrounded by a layer of tissue called the **perimysium**; within each fascicle are about 150 myofibers lying parallel to each other, which are covered by a layer of connective tissue called the **endomysium**.

Within each myofiber is a structured system of organelles (the tiny "organs" of each cell) that make up the foundation for the muscle to work. And within each myofiber are multiple threads of myofibrils that contain **actin** and **myosin** filaments.

Almost all cells of the body have one nucleus (the control center of every cell), but myofibers contain more than one. Within each myofiber is the sarcoplasmic reticulum, which stores calcium until it is needed for muscle contraction.

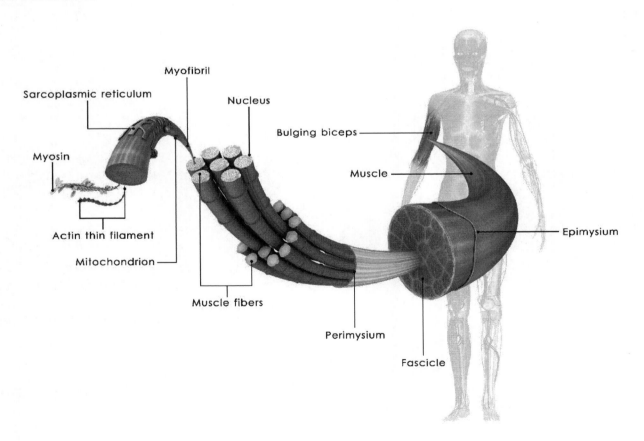

Draw it out! Try your hand at reproducing these and all the images found in this section—it will help you remember the information better. First, study the image, noting the different parts of the drawing and their names. Then, either trace or look off of the image to create a duplicate. *Then,* once you are feeling confident with the information, try to draw it from memory.

The two types of proteins which we just mentioned are:

1. Myosin: a large protein usually called the thick filament.

2. Actin: a smaller protein usually called the thin filament.

These proteins are organized into thin and thick **filaments** (long chains of subunit proteins) which repeat along the length of the myofibril in sections called sarcomeres. Myofilament is the term for the chains of (primarily) actin and myosin that pack a muscle fiber. These are the force-generating structures. Muscles contract by sliding the thin (actin) and thick (myosin) filaments along each other.

Sliding Filament Theory
Understanding muscle structure and movement can aid trainers in developing safe and effective strength programs for clients.

Sliding filament theory explains how muscles contract, relax, and produce force. Muscle fibers are comprised of myofibrils, smaller fibers. Myofibrils are themselves made up of actin, or thin, proteins and myosin, or thick, filaments. As filaments slide in and out, the muscle contracts.

The amount of tension a muscle can generate depends on its length: this is the **length-tension relationship**. When a muscle experiences tension, it will contract or lengthen; how much it will do so depends on the amount of force the muscle is able to generate. A muscle will be unable to produce enough force to contract if it is lengthened to excess.

A *repetition* in a muscle exercise includes three separate phases:

- Concentric phase (the process of lifting the weight).
- Transition or peak contraction phase (mid-point).
- Eccentric phase (the process of lowering the weight).

During the **concentric** phase, the muscle shortens (contracts); during the **eccentric** phase, it lengthens.

> For example: During a squat exercise, as the body descends into the squat, gluteus maximus enters the eccentric phase. The gluteus maximus shortens during the ascent from the squat position, entering the concentric phase; at this time, the gluteus maximus acts as the prime mover.

The mechanism that allows the muscle to contract and relax is called **cross-bridge cycling.** Cross-bridge cycling is the production of movement and the generation of force by muscle cells.

Skeletal Muscle and the CNS
The brain and spinal cord make up the **CNS** (the central nervous system). They control the body's activity and movement, acting as processing centers for the whole nervous system.

Action potentials—calls for specific functions—are sent from the CNS to stimulate the whole muscle for movement; the muscle fibers are then activated by a motor unit. Muscle fibers contract at the command of a motor nerve or motor unit. A **motor unit** is defined as a motor nerve and all the specific muscle fibers it innervates or activates.

When the muscle fibers' T-tubules are excited by an action potential, the inner portion of the muscle fiber is depolarized and muscle contraction starts to take place. The calcium that is stored inside the sarcoplasmic reticulum is released into the cell's **cytosol**, the liquid portion of the cell that is outside the nucleus.

Calcium is like a messenger. Once calcium is inside the cytosol, it looks for troponin and binds to it. When calcium is bonded to the regulatory filament troponin it causes the other regulatory filament, tropomyosin, to change shape.

The regulatory filaments troponin and tropomyosin are part of the thin filament actin. When tropomyosin is changing shape, active sites on actin are exposed. Myosin contains cross-bridge heads; when the active sites on actin are exposed, these cross-bridge heads will bind to them.

To contract a muscle, ATP causes a power stroke within the cross-bridge. That power stroke occurs as actin is pulled inward toward the center of the sarcomere. Actin and myosin are pulled towards each other, causing the sliding action. The muscle fiber will then shorten and generate force, causing muscle contraction.

Muscles stay contracted as long as calcium stays within the cytosol. Once calcium is pumped back into the sarcoplasmic reticulum from the calcium pump, myosin cross-bridge heads are broken from the active sites on actin. Tropomyosin will then cover these binding sites, and muscle relaxation can take place.

Cardiac Muscle
The difference between skeletal and cardiac muscle lies within their names. Skeletal muscle is attached to the skeletal structure and allows for the body's movement. Skeletal muscle is striated and is **voluntary** muscle.

Cardiac muscle, on the other hand, is the muscle that makes up the heart. Cardiac muscle is **involuntary**, which means self-contracting. Cardiac muscle is striated just like skeletal muscle.

Muscle Fibers
There are three types of muscle fibers in the human body: **Type I fibers, Type IIB, and Type IIA fibers**; each type of fiber serves a purpose, from holding our head up to sprinting around a track.

1. **Type I fibers** are **slow twitch fibers**; these fibers are most resistant to fatigue. They produce large amounts of ATP through the oxidative system. Type I fibers are developed through training and genetics. They are found in postural muscles, such as the neck and spine; they are also found in large amounts in marathon runners.

2. **Type IIB fibers** are **fast twitch fibers**; these fibers can produce bursts of power, but they fatigue quickly. ATP produced in the nonoxidative system is broken down rapidly in these fibers. These fibers are found in large amounts in sprinters.

3. **Type IIA fibers** are a combination of Type I and Type II fibers. ATP is produced in both the aerobic and anaerobic systems; Type IIA fibers can produce fast and strong muscle contractions.

Even though these fibers are a combination of both Type I and Type II, they are still more prone to fatigue than Type I. Resistance training can turn Type IIB fibers into Type IIA fibers.

Muscle Classifications

Each muscle produces an action by attaching to a proximal and distal end of a bone. For every joint to be movable, there have to be two opposing muscle groups: an agonist and an antagonist.

An **agonist** is a prime mover that moves part of the body in one direction. **Antagonists** are the prime movers that move that body part it in the opposite direction. Muscles never work alone; when the agonist muscle is contracting the antagonist to that muscle is relaxing.

For example: When elbow flexion is taking place, the bicep (the agonist) will be contracting while the triceps will be relaxing (the antagonists). When elbow extension is taking place, the triceps (the antagonists) will be contracting and the bicep (the agonist) will be relaxing.

Concentric contractions are when the muscle shortens when contracting. (Example: The upward phase of a bicep curl.)

Eccentric contractions are when the muscle lengthens when contracting. (Example: The downward phase of a bicep curl.)

Isometric contractions occur when the muscle is neither shortening nor lengthening. (Example: Curling a dumbbell half way up and holding it in fixed position.)

Body Planes and Axes

When considering body movement, keep in mind that there are three body planes, referred to as the cardinal planes:

1. **Sagittal Plane**: This vertical plane divides the body into left and right sides.

2. **Transverse**: This horizontal plane divides the body into upper (superior) and lower (inferior) portions.

3. **Frontal (Coronal)**: This vertical plane divides the body into front (anterior) and back (posterior) portions.

These planes allow for human movement around an axis. An **axis** is a straight line around which an object rotates. Movement at the joint takes place in a plane about an axis. There are three axes of rotation.

1. **Mediolateral axis** lies perpendicular to the sagittal plane.

2. **Anteroposterior axis** lies perpendicular to the frontal plane.

3. **Longitudinal axis** lies perpendicular to the transverse plane.

Movements and Examples

The **sagittal plane** allows flexion and extension movement. It rotates around the mediolateral axis. Some examples of this kind of movement would be walking or squatting.

The **frontal plane** allows for abduction/adduction, side flexion, and inversion/eversion. It rotates around the anteroposterior axis. Side bending and lateral arm lefts are examples of this kind of movement.

The **transverse plane** allows internal and external rotation, horizontal flexion and extension, and supination and pronation. It rotates around the longitudinal axis. This movement allows for activities such as throwing a baseball or performing a golf swing.

Anatomical Position
The body is standing erect and facing forward, with the arms at the sides and palms facing forward. The legs are parallel, and the toes are pointed forward.

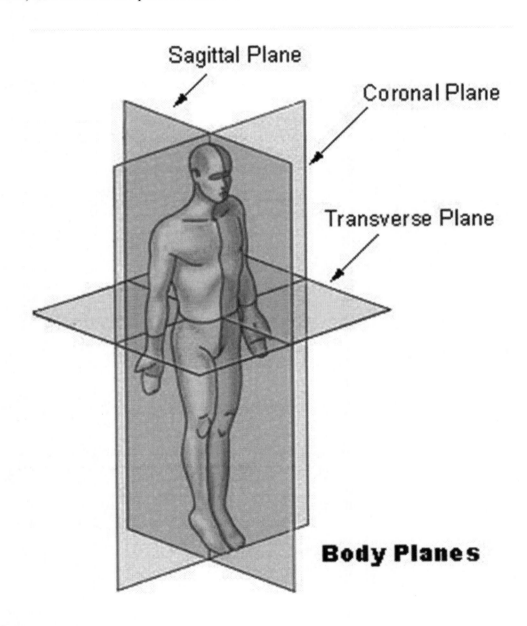

Body Planes

Anatomical Directions
     Proximal: Nearest to the body center.

Distal: Away from the body center.

Superior (cranial): Towards the head.

Inferior (caudal): Towards the feet.

Anterior (ventral): Towards the front.

Posterior (dorsal): Towards the back.

Medial: Closer to the midline.

Lateral: Away from the midline.

Joints

Joints are where two bones meet. The joints hold the bones together and allow mobility within the skeletal structure. Joints have three classifications:

1. **Fixed Joints (fibrous joints)**: Joints that have no movement. They are held together with fibrous (high strength) connective tissue. You will find these joints in the sutures of the skull. These immovable joints are also classified as **synarthrosis**.

2. **Slightly Movable Joints (cartilaginous joints)**: Joints found in the vertebrae of the spine and the ribcage. The vertebrae are connected to each other by cartilage pads which allows for slight movement. These slightly movable joints are also classified as **amphiarthrosis.**

3. **Freely Movable Joints (synovial joints)**: The most common joints found in the body. These joints allow the head to move from side to side, the knee and elbow to bend, and the shoulder to rotate. Freely movable joints are also classified as **diarthrosis.**

There are six different types of synovial joints in the human body.

Ball and socket joints allow circumduction, rotation, and angular movements in all planes (for example, the shoulder and hip joints).

Hinge joints allow the movements of flexion and extension in one plane (for example, the knee and elbow joints).

Pivot joints allow for rotation around a central axis. This allows range of motion of the head and stability of the neck.

Saddle joints allow movement of flexion, extension, abduction, adduction, and circumduction and opposition (for example, the thumb joint).

Gliding joints allow for inversion and eversion (for example, the ankle joint).

Condyloid joints allow for circumduction, abduction, adduction, flexion, and extension (for example, the wrist joint).

Synovial joints contain articular cartilage, ligaments, synovial cavity, bursa, and joint capsules. All of these aspects allow the bones different ranges of motion.

When two bones conjoin together to form a synovial joint, the end surfaces of the bones are covered in articular cartilage. **Articular cartilage** is smooth and healthy tissue that allows joints to move easier; this allows bones to glide over each other with less friction.

Ligaments are the connective tissues which hold bones together. They can be found on the outside or inside of the joint cavity.

The joint capsule is a fibrous connective tissue that seals the joint space like an envelope. The joint capsule provides stability to the joint and surrounds the synovial cavity.

Synovial fluid is a lubricant inside the joint capsule. It is concealed by the synovial membrane. Synovial fluid's job is to cushion joints and make it easier for bones and cartilage to move past each other.

The Bursa is a sac filled with fluid that minimizes friction absorbs shock.

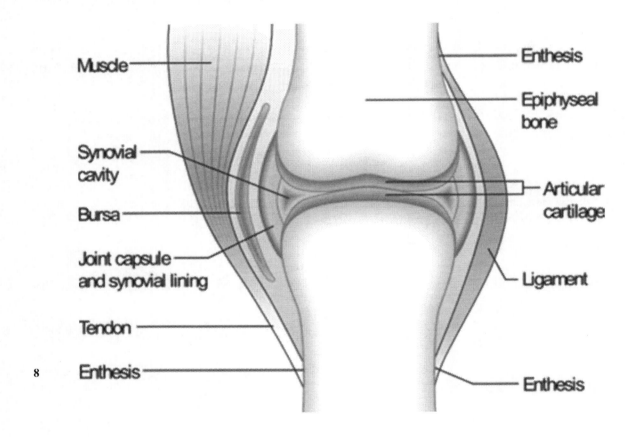

Movements around a Joint

There are many terms that explain movements around a joint. These terms are:

---

[8] By Madhero88 (Own work) [CC BY-SA 3.0 (http://creativecommons.org/licenses/by-sa/3.0)], via Wikimedia Commons.

1. **Flexion**: Movement that decreases the joint angle.

2. **Extension:** Movement that increases the joint angle.

3. **Adduction**: Movement toward the midline of the body.

4. **Abduction**: Movement away from the midline of the body.

5. **Rotation**: Movement either toward the midline or away from the midline of the body.

6. **Circumduction**: A combination of flexion, extension, abduction, and adduction movements.

7. **Supination**: Rotational movement at the radioulnar joint in the wrist. (Rotating the palm face up.)

8. **Pronation**: Rotational movement at the radioulnar joint in the wrist. (Rotating the palm face down.)

9. **Inversion**: Turning the sole of the foot toward the midline of the body.

10. **Eversion**: Turning the sole of the foot away from the midline of the body.

The following diagrams show these movements. Try them out yourself to get an idea of how they feel.

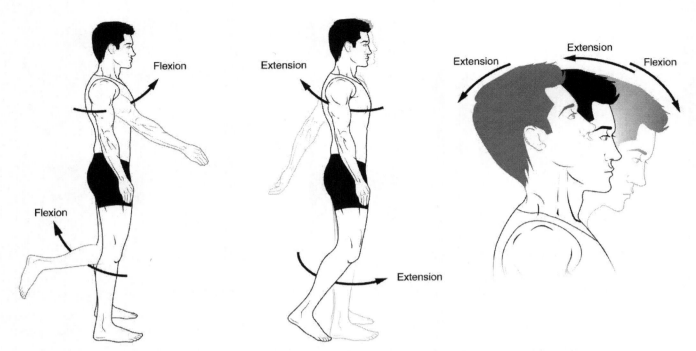

(a) and (b) Angular movements: flexion and extension at the shoulder and knees

(c) Angular movements: flexion and extension of the neck

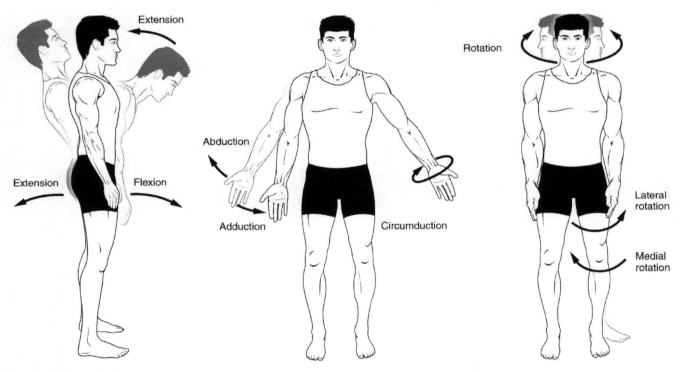

(d) Angular movements: flexion and extension of the vertebral column

(e) Angular movements: abduction, adduction, and circumduction of the upper limb at the shoulder

(f) Rotation of the head, neck, and lower limb

9

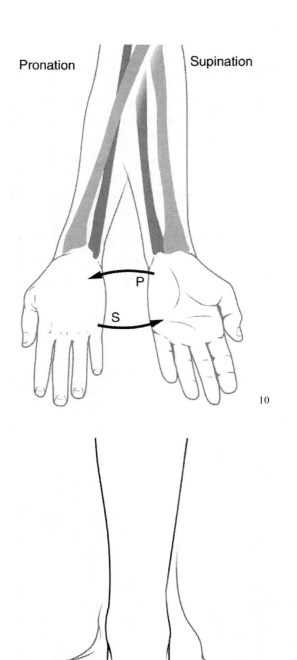

Pronation   Supination

P

S

10

Inversion   Eversion

11

[10] "Pronation and supination" by Connexions - http://cnx.org. Licensed under CC BY 3.0 via Commons - https://commons.wikimedia.org/wiki/File:Pronation_and_supination.jpg#/media/File:Pronation_and_supination.jpg

[11] "Eversion and inversion" by Connexions - http://cnx.org. Licensed under CC BY 3.0 via Commons - https://commons.wikimedia.org/wiki/File:Eversion_and_inversion.jpg#/media/File:Eversion_and_inversion.jpg

Proper Form and Techniques

Training with proper technique is incredibly important in all areas of personal training and exercise. Lifting and lowering the weights with complete control in a slow manner are critical. For example, when performing shoulder exercises, the eccentric phase, the muscles are lengthening during resistance. The muscles in the shoulder and rotator cuff are subject to extreme forces if the exercises are not performed correctly.

Proper technique and form are critical when lifting weights to reduce the risk of injury.

For example, the Standing Dumbbell Shoulder Press:

The standing iso-lateral (meaning one side at a time) dumbbell shoulder press is an excellent exercise to strengthen the shoulders, as well as to work the core muscles.

- Stand with feet together and knees slightly bent.
- Hold each dumbbell 90 degrees to the side of each shoulder with palms facing forward.
- Draw in the core muscles and contract the gluteus maximus muscles.
- Press the dumbbells to the ceiling and lower back down to the original position.

Shoulders must remain level during the entire set. If that is not possible, lighter weights must be used. For more of a challenge, have your client stand on a BOSU ball.

The Most Important Step of Prevention and Correction is Detection

Neutral Spine
Neutral spine is defined as the natural position of the spine when all parts of the body are in good alignment. In the neutral spine position, the pelvis is neutral while the natural curves of the back are maintained.

Proper Posture and Movement
In a neutral spine position, the body is balanced and is able to function at its strongest. Stress to the vertebrae, muscles, joints, and tissues are minimized. This helps to reduce the risk of injury while increasing the efficiency of movement for each exercise. It is important to view the body as an integrated unit when performing exercises, rather than as a multitude of individual parts or muscles. Watch for any imbalances—they can lead to chronic pain or injury. Exercising in neutral spine should make the movements more challenging. This is a good thing! We want to work hard, and above all we want to work our bodies in a safe and correct manner.

How to Find Neutral Spine
Find a wall and ask your client to stand with their feet shoulder width apart without locking their knees. His head, shoulder, and back should be up against the wall with heels about two inches from the baseboard. Have him draw in his abdominal muscles, decreasing the arch in his lower back. Ask him to step away from the wall while keeping his body in an upright, vertical alignment. This will show you, and your client, what the perfect posture and neutral spine are for his body.

Static Verses Dynamic Posture

Static Posture
Static posture refers to the body's alignment when it is still. Static posture results from the length-tension relationships of the muscles to the joints. Problems with static posture may be indicative of current or future problems with posture in general. Furthermore, poor static posture can affect dynamic posture (see below).

Dynamic Posture

Dynamic posture refers to the bodily alignment that results from the length-tension relationships between working and opposing muscles during movement. While performing repetitive movements during exercise (and at other times), being mindful of maintaining proper dynamic posture is essential. Poor dynamic posture can impact static posture.

Muscle Imbalances
A sedentary lifestyle is one of the major causes of muscle imbalance, where muscles become shorter or longer than they should be. Particularly in a sedentary lifestyle, certain muscles become tight or shortened from sitting for long periods of time. This affects the opposing muscle and causes problems in the musculoskeletal system. Here are some of the more common problems with posture:

Tight Hip Flexors can cause many problems with posture, because the human body is meant to be upright most of the time, not seated at a desk all day. The hip flexors become shortened due to sitting for long periods of time. This can cause the pelvis to rotate anteriorly or tilt downward in front.

As a result, the **lumbar spine becomes arched** and the **thoracic spine develops a hunch back** alignment. You may also gain a **forward head posture** when sitting for too long at a desk.

Tight hip flexors make it impossible for the abdominal muscles to work. This makes it difficult to achieve benefit from an abdominal workout. To make up for the weak hip extensors, the **hamstrings may take over the work, increasing their risk for injury** due to **excessive strain** which was originally meant for the glutes.

Here are two different ways in which you can begin to correct your muscle imbalances and posture problems:

Self-Myofascial Release
This may sound more complicated than it really is. *Myo* means muscle and *fascial* means the tissue that surrounds the muscles. Repeated muscle contractions can develop adhesions of tension in the muscle. This tension can be released through a deep tissue massage, which is best done by a professional. You or your client can spend the hourly rate to get the client's muscles worked on by a therapist. If that's not an option, then you yourself can attempt to massage them by using a foam roller, a medicine ball, or even a tennis ball. This can be done before or after a workout and should focus on those muscles causing posture problems and imbalances. Use the foam roller before you perform your stretching and flexibility routine.

Begin by placing the part of the body that needs massaging on the roller, keeping the muscle relaxed as much as possible while applying pressure to its entire length. You may notice that some spots hurt the client more than others. Spend about twenty seconds applying pressure to those tender spots.

Each time you perform this massage, you should notice less tension in the muscle. Over time, those tender spots will seem to disappear.

Increased Flexibility Training

Undergoing such flexibility exercises as yoga or Pilates can have an extremely beneficial effect on muscle imbalances and posture problems. Stretching increases both the flexibility of the muscles along with their strength, and the various poses in yoga will help work out any existing imbalances. Recommend that your client begin a stretching routine, one which pays equal attention to all parts of the body (or, specifically those parts requiring correction) or have her enroll in a flexibility-specific class, such as yoga.

Activities of Daily Living (ADL)

Activities of daily living involve maintaining a continued wellbeing, along with keeping good personal hygiene, eating nutritious meals, and performing standard feats of mobility. Staying active and healthy depends upon having actively healthy lungs, muscles, joints, and cardiovascular functions.

Regular physical activity makes certain activities of daily living—such as eating, dressing, walking, going up the stairs, getting in and out of bed, grocery shopping, doing housework, playing with grandchildren, etc.—much easier. It is important to understand that strength and flexibility are not things to be considered only when exercising. They are essential components of life, and without them, many of our daily activities would be close to impossible.

Considerations When Designing an Exercise Prescription

For every facet of fitness, and for each goal set by either yourself or your client, there is an appropriate frequency, intensity, time, and type (**FITT**) of exercise to be used.

With a client who is just beginning to exercise, it is important to monitor intensity and progress. A popular method of monitoring these factors is the Borg scale. Clients may describe their level of exertion according to the Borg scale as follows:

- 6 – 7: no exertion at all
- 7.5 – 8: extremely light
- 9 – 10: very light
- 11 – 12: light
- 13 – 14: somewhat hard
- 15 – 16: hard (heavy)
- 17 – 18: very hard
- 19: extremely hard
- 20: maximal exertion

Clients should perform aerobic activities like walking and cycling at level 13 (somewhat hard).

Clients should perform strength activities such as squats or lifting weights at levels 15 – 17 (hard to very hard). As a client's fitness increases, increase the intensity of the strength training.

Generally, challenging activities become easier over time; therefore clients score these exercises lower on the Borg scale than they would have when first beginning to perform them. For example, a client may consider slow walking on a treadmill to be level 13 on the Borg scale when beginning training. However, as fitness levels improve, it may be necessary to add an incline to the treadmill to get that same level-13 effort.

Physiological Considerations for Adolescents:

1. Higher maximal and submaximal oxygen uptake (VO2max), resulting in increased oxygen delivery. This corresponds with growth spurt, resulting from hypertrophy of the heart and stimulation of red blood cells and hemoglobin.

2. Higher resting and exercising heart rates.

3. Lower resting and exercising blood pressures.

4. Hormonal changes.

5. Thermoregulatory differences, resulting in reduced sweating rate and higher heat production and increased sensitivity to excessive heat and cold.

6. Musculoskeletal and Bone Formation.

7. Body Composition.

The following considerations also need to be included:

Physical Considerations for Adolescents

1. Existing medical conditions

   - Asthma: A chronic respiratory disorder characterized by recurrent breathing difficulties and bronchial spasms; can be exacerbated by exercise.

   - Epilepsy: A common and diverse set of chronic neurological disorder characterized by seizures.

   - Diabetes: A chronic disease in which there are increased levels of sugar in the blood.

2. Overuse injuries due to: inadequate warm-up, improper footwear, poor technique, faulty equipment, or overtraining.

3. Appropriateness of resistance training

   - Strict Supervision is required.

- Sports/Activity Specific.

- Focus on proper technique by starting with body weight resistance exercise (push-ups) and progressing to using light weights with frequent repetitions.

Psychological Considerations for Adolescents

1. Healthy Body Image: one important source of self-esteem for youth is a healthy body image. Peer pressure and other social influences shape how youth perceive themselves, and participation in healthy behaviors like proper nutrition and exercise can reinforce the idea that health is more important than appearance.

2. Mental Discipline (parents and coaches need to be on the lookout for the following states):

   - State anxiety: State anxiety is a stress reaction that occurs during sport/recreation preparation.

   - Trait anxiety: Trait anxiety is an intrinsic personality characteristic that may be compounded in situation stress (worry, self-criticism, and anxiety).

   - Burn-out: Emotional fatigue and isolation, accompanied by sub-par physical performance, burn-out indicates stress from training and competition.

3. Social Skills: Spontaneous interaction with their peers gives children the chance to experience teamwork and compromise, and to develop social skills and effective communication. Group physical activity and play offers children these opportunities.

4. Lifestyle Attitudes: Participation in sports and recreational physical activity has numerous benefits that can be seen in young age groups. It helps youth develop coping and decision making skills for the competitive world and teaches them how to attempt to achieve realistic personal goals. Structured activities set the foundation for challenges that motivate children and youth towards cooperation and self-gratification.

Current research data does not allow recognition of a certain minimal level of daily physical activity; however, a reasonable goal is for children to engage in at least a moderate level of activity for thirty to sixty minutes on most days of the week. As there are no evidence-based standard approaches to improving exercise habits in this demographic, the following models can be used:

1. Adult Prescription Model: Activity is performed for a number of minutes, three to five times a week. Examples include walking or biking.

2. Exercise "Menu": A list of possible activities is presented, based off of the child's interest and the feasibility within the community. Examples include team sports, recreational activities, and activity clubs.

3. Increasing Lifestyle Activities: No structured activity, simply an increase in everyday activities to increase caloric expenditure. Examples include using the stairs instead of escalator or elevator, or walking or riding a bike instead of driving or being driven to a destination.

4. Decreasing Sedentary Time: Reducing the amount of time watching TV or playing video games.

Children ages five to twelve should engage in an accumulation of at least sixty minutes or more of age-appropriate activity on all or most days of the week. Physical activity should range from moderate to vigorous intermittently throughout the duration of play or exercise; ideally, children should engage in several periods of physical activity or play for fifteen minutes or more each day throughout the day. Specific age-appropriate activities should be designed for optimal health, wellness, and performance benefits. Children and adolescents should avoid extended periods of inactivity (two hours or more), particularly during the daytime.

Exercise Prescription for Children & Adolescents

Aerobic Activity

- Frequency: 5 - 7 days a week.

- Intensity: Moderate to vigorous activity that is intermittent in nature.

- Time: 60 minutes or more/day; should be in several sessions of 15 – 20 minutes.

- Type: Age-appropriate exercise that utilizes all muscle groups (running, swimming, etc.).

Resistance Training

- Frequency: 5 – 7 days a week.

- Intensity: 4 – 6 muscle groups; 1 – 3 sets of 8 – 15 repetitions for each group.

- Time: 20 – 30 minutes for each session. Add weight gradually up to a max of 6 reps; add 1 – 2 reps per session up to a max of 12 – 15 reps.

- Type: Submaximal resistance; make use of full range of motion.

Flexibility Activity

- Frequency: 5 – 7 days a week.

- Intensity: Light to moderate; 12 – 13 on the Borg scale.

- Time: Each stretch should be held for 15 – 30 seconds.

- Type: 2 – 4 static stretches for each muscle group.

Exercise for Older Adults

The majority of adults become less physically active with age, increasing their risk of developing a number of chronic disease states. Of people aged sixty-five and over, only about twenty-one percent engage in regular activity. The benefits of exercise for adults in this age group include:

- Slowed changes in physiological age that decrease exercise capacity.

- Improved ability to cope with age-related changes in body composition.

- Improved cognitive and psychological well-being.

- Ameliorated management of chronic disease.

- Reduced risk of physical impairment.

- Increased longevity.

A comprehensive pre-exercise clinical evaluation should include a medical history, physical exam, and certain laboratory tests in order to identify:

- Medical contraindications to exercise.

- Risks of disease where exercise testing is needed prior to starting an exercise program.

- Clinical significant disease states that would require an individual to participate in a medically supervised exercise programs.

- Special needs and considerations.

Physiological Considerations

1. Lower maximum and sub-maximum oxygen uptake, due to reduced maximum heart rate and cardiac output.

2. Higher resting and exercising blood pressures.

3. Decreased immune function.

4. Decreased sensitivity in thermoregulation, resulting in reduced total body water and reduced capacity for sweating.

5. Increase in risk factors, such as

    - Hypertension: High blood pressure.

    - Hyperlipidemia: Increased blood cholesterol levels.

    - Diabetes: A chronic disease in which there are increased levels of sugar in the blood.

78

- Coronary artery disease: A narrowing of the small blood vessels that supply blood and oxygen to the heart.

Physical Considerations

1. Decrease in bone and muscle mass.

2. Decreased balance and coordination.

3. Increase in obesity; higher percentage of fat mass.

4. Osteoarthritis: degenerative arthritis or degenerative joint disease.

5. Orthopedic injuries.

Psychological Considerations

1. Self-efficacy: Research shows that exercise improves many older adults' perception of their ability to perform the tasks needed to achieve personal goals. Evidence further shows that this improvement in self-efficacy is critical for decreasing functional decline and impairment.

2. Self-concept: An individual's perception of him- or herself—self-esteem—develops from the validation of his or her value, use, and competency. Changes in self-esteem among the aging may accompany age-related changes in social and familial roles, in lifestyle, and in activities.

3. Cognitive functioning: Physical fitness has beneficial effects on cognitive functioning.

4. Life satisfaction: Older adults who exercise regularly tend to demonstrate a more positive attitude toward work and are generally healthier. There is also a strong correlation between activity levels and self-reported happiness.

Exercise Prescription Guidelines for Older Adults

Aerobic Activity

- Frequency: 5 – 7 days a week.

- Intensity: Light to moderate; 50 – 80% of maximum HR.

- Time: 30 – 60 minutes a day (can be in 10 – 15 minute intervals).

- Type: Walking, stationary bicycling; low orthopedic stress.

Resistance Training[12]

- Frequency: 2 days a week.

- Intensity: 1 set of 8 – 10 repetitions for each muscle group; Borg scale: 12 – 13

---

[12] Older adults should be discouraged from strength/resistance training during active periods of pain or inflammation.

- Time: 20 – 30 minutes a session; add weight gradually as tolerated.

- Type: Weight training machines; tubing & bands (with assistance).

Flexibility Activity

- Frequency: 5 – 7 days a week.

- Intensity: Light to moderate; 12 – 13 on the Borg scale.

- Time: Each stretch should be held for 15 – 30 seconds.

- Type: 2 – 4 static stretches for each muscle group.

TRAINING

A **well-developed exercise program** is vital to meeting the needs of participating clients. Exercise prescriptions must address the client's needs, interests, and limitations; and, perhaps most importantly, they must enhance health through disease prevention, producing a change in the personal health behavior of an individual with continuous physical activity.

When designing an appropriate exercise prescription, you need to take into account five essential components: **mode, intensity, duration, frequency, and progression.**

1. **Mode**: The type of activity or exercise within which the client will participate.

2. **Frequency**: How often, per week, the client will be participating in each exercise or activity.

3. **Intensity**: How hard the client's body works during the activity. A client's health and fitness goals and current level of fitness determine ideal exercise intensity. Exercise intensity can be measured by the client's **target heart rate**; the **talk test**, or the ability to comfortably maintain a conversation while performing the exercise at a certain intensity; and the **rate of perceived exertion scale**—the **Borg scale**, discussed above.

   Heart rate increases with the intensity of an exercise; in fact, the heart can be considered a built-in system that measures exercise intensity. Target Heart Rate (THR) range allows you to track and guide a client's exercise intensity.

   When engaging in moderate physical activity, an individual's THR should be fifty to seventy percent of their maximum heart rate. To estimate a person's maximum heart rate, subtract his or her age from 220 beats per minute (bpm). Keep in mind, however, that this is only an estimated value; use this method with caution.

4. **Duration**: How the long the activity or exercise session will last.

5. **Progression**: Changing your client's workouts to be effective and challenging.

When designing an exercise program, a health fitness professional should monitor the client's progress, keeping records of the client's adaption. The program should be dynamic, growing as the client adapts, in order to maintain exercise **consistency**, which helps achieve ongoing fitness results. Commitment to a regular workout regimen increases fitness level, improves health, and generates a greater sense of mental well-being.

There are five exercise principles of which a health fitness professional should have a good understanding before designing an exercise program for their client. They are: **specificity, adaptation, overload, reversibility,** and **progression**.

1. **The Specificity Principle**

   Exercising a specific body part may affect the body elsewhere, but it *primarily* develops the part in question. Therefore, to see improvement in any activity or skill, that specific activity or skill must be exercised regularly. A runner should train by running, a swimmer by swimming, and a cyclist by cycling. While general conditioning routines are helpful for improving overall fitness, it is necessary to prescribe area-specific training for a client to improve in one particular area.

2. **The Adaptation Principle**

   The human body is adaptable: it can adjust as demands on it increase or decrease. People can develop muscle coordination and sports-specific skills by practicing the activity repeatedly; it will become easier to perform. Those new to exercise will be sore after starting a new routine, but muscle soreness will decrease after repetition over weeks and months, due to adaptation.

3. **The Principle of Overload**

   In order for adaptation to occur, more stress than normal is necessary. To improve fitness, workload must be increased.

   For muscles to become stronger, they must gradually work harder, working against a load greater than to which they have become habituated. For increased endurance, muscles must work for longer time periods or at a higher intensity.

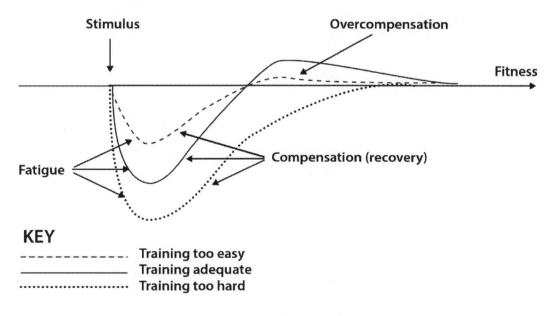

Different training loads have different effects on the athlete's recovery

In order to continue achieving new levels of fitness and move beyond plateaus, one must regularly make adjustments to the training load. Remember the variables of FITT (frequency, intensity, time, and type): all of those can be adjusted with regard to the training load. Of course, a training load that is too drastic or too advanced can result in injury, so always exercise good judgment.

In order to create a progressive training overload, consider the following variables of exercise program design:

Intensity: The amount of resistance or load used in an exercise: this is expressed as a percentage of one-repetition maximum (1RM).

Exercise Selection: The specific movements prescribed.

Repetitions: The complete range of motion (ROM) of the lengthening and shortening phase of the muscle action, expressed as the number of times the complete cycle is performed.

Sets: How many repetitions of an exercise are completed at one time.

Tempo: The velocity of the movement of the exercise.

Rest Interval: The recovery period between exercises during which muscles refuel and prepare to carry out more work. Load and training outcome determine the length of the rest interval. Load has a proportional relationship with rest period: the greater the load, the longer the rest period necessary for the muscle to restore its energy pathways.

4. **The Principle of Reversibility**
Aptly described as the "use it or lose it" principle, the Principle of Reversibility states that any gains made through training can be lost once that training is ceased. Similarly, detraining or deconditioning effects can be reversed once one begins to train again.

5. **The Principle of Progression**
According to this principle, an optimal level of overload should be achieved within an optimal timeframe. Gradually increasing workload over time will improve fitness with minimal risk of injury. Overload that is too slow will not stimulate improvement; however, overload at too rapid a rate may cause injury or damage to the muscle. For instance, an athlete who only exercises vigorously on weekends is violating the principle of progression, is unlikely to see obvious fitness gains, and may be at risk of injury.

Another important element of this principle is adequate rest and recovery in order to avoid exhaustion and injury from continuous stress. An athlete who trains hard all the time risks overtraining, injury, and even a decrease in fitness.

Improving the Quality of Life

There are multiple principles, in addition to those listed above, which can and should be utilized to improve fitness and quality of life.

Principle of Individualism

Everyone will respond to exercise differently. The individual response will be shaped by inherent capabilities, hereditary, nutrition habits, past injuries or illness, sleep patterns, etc.

Physiological factors will also have a significant impact on training. The body's physiological readiness for exercise tends to vary by age. Individuals sharing a chronological age may differ in their levels of maturity; furthermore, they may be up to four years apart in developmental and biological age. **Chronological age** refers to the years since birth. **Biological age** is one's age based on the stage of development, and is often measured by skeletal age or physique maturity.

However, there is also a third type of again, **training age**, which is determined by how long the person has been training. Training age can be broken down into three aspects:

- Sports Specific: The length of time one has competed in a sport.
- General: The length of time one has been training or working out.
- Lifestyle: A common measure of how active one is on a daily basis.

Thus, athletes sharing a biological age likely have the same training age and can train accordingly, even if their chronological ages differ. Likewise, athletes at the same chronological age may have different training ages if their biological ages differ; training should be adjusted appropriately.

Principle of Variety

Too often training becomes tedious. This can be prevented by infusing variety into a training program. Varying the approach, the activity, the intensity and the duration of a training program can keep boredom at bay. People are more likely to stick with a training program that offers variety and is interesting. Such programs often motivate the participant to work harder and therefore reach their training goals.

Principle of Active Involvement

This principle refers to one's willingness and personal commitment to a workout program, wherein, they are active participants in their own success. A long-term commitment is needed to ensure one successfully achieves their fitness goals. All aspects of one's life must contribute to the success or failure of the training program. Maintaining a positive attitude is a must. Conscientious participation in training is attained through communication between the coach and athlete or the trainer and the participant. The two collaborate to identify training objectives and plan long and short-term training programs.

ACE IFT Model

The American Council on Exercise (ACE) Integrated Fitness Training Model revolves around four phases: stability and mobility, movement training, load training, and performance training; these phases allow for integrated and multidimensional program design giving participants the opportunity to adapt with each level. The following is a summary of the Model; consult with ACE for details.

Phase One: Stability and Mobility

Phase One emphasizes balance and core training. Here, confirm that participants are prepared for exercise by ensuring stability in the lumbar spine and other key locations in the body, as well as appropriate movement in central areas like the pelvis. Phase One ensures that the participant is ready to learn new movement at a low risk of injury while gaining optimum results.

Phase Two: Movement Training

Phase Two consists of aerobic interval training to improve participants' levels of fitness. Not only is aerobic efficiency improved, but training movement patterns are also refined, preparing the body to add resistance to movements.

Phase Three: Load Training

Load training is resistance training. A client with demonstrated stability and aerobic fitness may increase the intensity of his or her training by adding resistance. In this phase, those clients wishing to gain strength or tone muscles will begin to achieve those goals. Furthermore, load training aids weight loss.

Phase Four: Performance Training

Clients training for athletic events may require performance training. In performance training, the velocity of muscle-force production is improved by increasing the velocity of the stretch-shorten cycle. This decreases the time spent in the **amortization phase**. During the amortization phase, the body converts muscle lengthening to muscle shortening; reducing the time spent in this phase increases the potential generation of power by the muscle.

Training Guidelines for Health, Fitness, and Athletic Performance

Health

The Centers for Disease Control and Prevention recommends the following for those seeking to improve their overall health through exercise: begin slowly. Even though cardiac events such as a heart attack are unlikely during exercise, the risk does increase when one suddenly becomes more active than normal. Gradually increase the level of activity. The Mayo Clinic suggests at least two hours and thirty minutes a week of moderate aerobic activity, or one hour and fifteen minutes a week of vigorous aerobic activity—ideally spaced throughout the week. Those with chronic health conditions are advised to speak with their doctor to find out if the condition will limit activity. The primary goal is to be as active as safely possible.

Fitness

To increase overall fitness, one must engage in cardiovascular, strength, and flexibility training. Cardiovascular activity could include group fitness classes, jogging, swimming, power walking, cycling, etc. The goal should be to raise the heart rate into the target zone (fifty to eighty-five percent of your maximum) and maintain it for an extended period of time.

To improve muscular strength, endurance, and tone, one can use weight machines, free weights, resistance bands, medicine balls, or do calisthenics (such as push-ups and abdominal crunches). Again, it is important to gradually increase repetitions and resistance levels.

Flexibility is the normal extensibility of all soft tissues that allow the full range of motion for each joint. Many people overlook the importance of flexibility training, but it plays an important role in injury prevention. Flexibility can also decrease the occurrences of muscle imbalances, joint dysfunctions, and overuse injuries.

There are many different types of stretching, but the three we will focus on are static, ballistic, and PNF:

1. Static stretching is a very common technique used as a corrective measure. It is the process of passively taking a muscle to the point of tension and holding the stretch for ten to thirty seconds. This type of stretch allows the muscles to relax due to autogenetic inhibition and provide for better elongation of the muscle.

2. Ballistic stretching consists of uncontrolled bouncing, jerking, bobbing, or pulsing to achieve greater range of motion. This technique is *not* a preferred stretching technique due to its possible risk of injury and soreness. When ballistic stretching is performed, the stretch causes muscles to contract, leading to possible tearing of the muscle fibers.

3. PNF stands for Proprioceptive Neuromuscular Facilitation. This type of stretching was designed for the rehabilitation of patients. The main goal of this technique is to facilitate muscle relaxation and a fuller range of motion.

Athletic Performance
While athletes can benefit from continuous training and interval training, so too can those who have the appropriate level of fitness.

In **continuous training**, participants perform exercise at a steady, moderate intensity over a sustained period of time; this improves cardiovascular endurance, reduces body fat, and helps maintain high levels of fitness during the off season. Continuous training should be performed at **70%** of the maximum heart rate. Some examples of continuous training follow below.

Running at an easy pace of **50 – 60%** of maximum heart rate (20 to 36% of V02 Max) for at least 60 minutes. Running at this pace metabolizes fat and is helpful for joggers and ultra-distance runners.

Running at a slightly faster pace of **60 – 70%** of maximum heart rate (36 to 52% of V02 Max) for 45 to 90 minutes. Running at this pace burns both glycogen and fat and is helpful for marathon runners.

Running at a faster, aerobic pace of **70 – 80%** of maximum heart rate (52 to 68% of V02 Max) for 30 – 45 minutes. Running at this pace burns glycogen and is helpful for marathon runners and those seeking to run distances of ten kilometers.

Running at **80 – 90%** of maximum heart rate (68 – 83% of V02 Max) for only 10 – 20 minutes. Running at this pace is anaerobic and burns glycogen; this type of running is useful for marathoners and those training for distances of five kilometers. It improves lactate tolerance and removal and the cardiovascular system overall.

Running at **90 – 100%** of maximum heart rate (83 – 99% of V02 Max) for only one to five minutes. Running at this pace is anaerobic and burns glycogen; it improves both glycogen burning and lactate tolerance and removal.

Interval training involves spacing work and recovery periods, or short high-intensity bursts, with lighter recovery periods. The athlete will still work during the recovery phase, but at a much lower intensity level. This cycle gets repeated over a period of time. Interval training can be used with aerobic and anaerobic energy systems.

Developing Skills: Methods

Balance
Balance is the body's ability to maintain equilibrium while stationary or moving. According to the CDC, it is an essential part of physical fitness related to performance. Coordinating the sensory organs (the eyes, ears, and proprioceptive organs of the joints) allows a fit individual to maintain balance, or be able to prevent him- or herself from falling.

> **Static Balance**: Maintaining the center of mass above the supportive base in a stationary position.

> **Dynamic Balance**: Maintaining balance during body movement.

The U.S. Department of Health and Human Services' 2008 publication "Physical Activity Guidelines for Americans" recommends balance training at least three times a week for both inactive individuals as well as active adults ages sixty-five or older. Balance training reduces falls and ankle sprains.

Because muscle strength and flexibility affect balance, resistance training and stretching improve it; Pilates, yoga, tai chi, dance, and walking do, too. Further training modalities and tools enhance balance skills. Training should be progressive and the proprioceptive challenge should be adjusted over time.

Agility
Agility is the body's ability to efficiently and effectively start, stop, and change direction. Agility requires certain neuromuscular abilities: speed, or how quickly the body can move; strength, or the muscle's ability to overcome resistance; and coordination, combining bodily movement with the body's sensory functions.

Speed
Speed is the body's ability to move as fast as possible. Speed may be learned and developed through training; appropriate running mechanics increase speed so that maximum velocity may be achieved in the shortest time period.

Some common guidelines for speed training include varying intensity of training, consistent training, running hills, sprints, core strengthening, and plyometrics.

Power
The body's ability to produce the most force in the shortest time period is called power. Power may be expressed by this equation:

$$\text{force (weight)} * \text{velocity}$$

Essentially, the equation expresses how fast weight is moved. An increase in any one of these variables results in an increase in power.

Power training should be part of any strength program and may consist of one to three sets per exercise. Use light to moderate loading: thirty to sixty percent of one repetition maximum (RM) for upper body exercises, and zero to sixty percent of one RM for lower body exercises. Repeat for three to six repetitions.

An athlete with more experience would begin by doing push-ups on the floor, progressing to power moves that would require propelling the body away from the floor with the maximum controlled strength and force. Intermediate-level power trainers should train three to four days a week.

Increasing the force component of the power equation requires heavy loading (85 – 100% of 1 RM); only athletes and others with extensive experience practice heavy loading. On the other hand, light-to-moderate loading (as described above) will increase response time if performed at an explosive velocity. Strength training programs should include multiple-set power programs (of three to six sets).

Coordination

Coordination expresses how well an individual controls his or her limbs. When the joints, muscles, and senses work well together, the limbs move smoothly and accurately. Usually at least two or more limbs are necessary to perform general activities like walking, lifting, sitting, driving, etc. Exercise and sports require a higher level of coordination between the hands, eyes, and feet.

Reaction Time

Reaction time describes how quickly an individual can react and change his or her body position using the maximum rate of force production, in any plane of motion and from all body positions. Practice, experience, coordination, and strength, among other factors, affect reaction time.

Drills to improve reaction time include:

- Basketball: one-on-one and wave drills

- Tennis: rapid fire volley drills

- Football: have linemen drop to the ground, then return to a starting position

- Swimming/track: starting drills

- Volleyball: rolling, recovering, digging, blocking, and sprawling drills

- Hockey/soccer: one-on-one defensive drills and short-range goal-defending drills

- Hockey: face-off drills

- Badminton: smash-return drills

EQUIPMENT

When working with equipment, either your own or that which belongs to a larger facility, you must understand the safety measures, capabilities, and proper uses of each piece of equipment. Of course, we can't cover every single piece of equipment that you may encounter in the world in this review, but we will go over those that you are more likely to encounter in the professional field.

Exercise equipment doesn't consist solely of physical weights or tools; audio/visual (A/V) equipment can be a substantial (but worthy) financial investment that provides multiple benefits to both the instructor and the participants. Professional AV equipment provides a quality sound experience while expanding music options. For instance, nowadays instructors can hook their iPhone to the stereo system to play a personalized playlist.

Types of Equipment

All equipment should be kept in good working condition and be properly stored to prevent injuries. Supervision is always recommended for new exercisers or for those progressing to new levels of intensity.

Steps
Steps should be sturdy, portable, and adjustable plastic benches without sharp edges. Those new to step should start with a low bench level, four to six inches in height, and progress to no more than twelve inches. Anything beyond this height will be strenuous and, depending on one's height, will likely pose a safety hazard. Steps are best used on a hardwood surface, though a carpeted floor can be used if absolutely necessary. A concrete surface should be avoided, as it is too hard on the joints. Steps are generally stackable, which makes storage easy.

Indoor Cycles
Classrooms for indoor group cycles can be arranged in various ways, depending on the size and shape of the space. Configuration options include: staggered rows, a half-circle, a circle, a U-shape, an alley way, or a half box. It is best to choose a configuration that will provide enough space for participants to maneuver safely on and off the bikes. Ideally, the bikes should be placed in such a manner to ensure that each participant has an unobstructed view of the instructor.

Medicine Balls
Ideally, at least twenty square feet of clutter-free space should be used when doing partner exercises with or tossing medicine balls. Ceilings should be high enough to accommodate moves such as overhead throws. Medicine balls should only be thrown against concrete or reinforced walls. Storing medicine balls in a bin or on racks is recommended.

Balance-Related Tools
The use of balance equipment should be based on fitness level and experience. Those who are less experienced should use such equipment under supervision and/or next to a support structure such as a sturdy chair for lateral stability. This type of equipment will increase the balance level, so if one has not mastered stability without the use of equipment (for example standing on one leg), they should not use equipment unsupervised. It is safer to store equipment like BOSUs, foam rollers, stability boards, and other balance tools away and out of the general exercise space.

Free Weights

It is best to create an organized free weight space away from cardio equipment and other highly-trafficked areas. The best storage options for free weights are a racking system or bins. Free weights can trip up people when left unattended, and can also be harmful if dropped. Arrange weights by size (lightest to heaviest). A mirror in front of the free weight space is ideal for self-monitoring. It's highly recommended that beginners, or those using particularly heavy loads, are spotted.

Elastic Resistance

Due to the light weight and thin structure of resistant tubing, elastic resistance materials tend to be one of the safer pieces of equipment. However, caution should still be exercised. Educate clients on the degrees of difficulty for resistance tubing. This is usually indicated by the color of the band, though standards differ slightly depending on the manufacturer. Elastic bands can snap with excessive pulling or stretching, which can cause injury. These bands can be easily hung on the wall for safe storage.

Stability Balls

Stability balls tend to take up a lot of space because of their round shape. Sizes can run from small (thirty centimeters) to extra-large (eighty-five centimeters). Be sure to properly inflate stability balls according to the manufacturer's guidelines. A clean, even surface is safest when using a stability ball. Sharp objects should never be in close proximity to stability balls. Supervision is highly recommended for beginners; using a wall or adjacent support structure as a brace is a good safety precaution. Storage options include elevated racks, netting, or bases made especially for stability balls. The following are guidelines from the American College of Sports Medicine for selecting the proper size stability ball:

Height	Size of Medicine Ball to Use
< 4'10"	30 – 35 cm
4'8" – 5'5"	45 cm
5'6" – 6'0"	55 cm
6'0" – 6'5"	65 cm
6'5"	75 cm
Long-legged or Heavier Exerciser	85 cm

Basic Components of a Session

While each session is individualized for specific requirements and preferences, there are some fitness components which apply across the board.

Warm-Up

The warm-up is generally understood to enhance overall performance and should always be the prerequisite for any physical activity. A good warm-up, five to ten minutes in duration, prepares the body for exercise by gradually raising the body temperature, increasing blood flow, and mentally preparing one for more vigorous activity. This limbers the muscles and prevents injury—it is never a good idea to leave out a warm-up. Jogging lightly in place, stretching out the muscles, or even walking are some examples of a basic warm-up, but it's recommended that you incorporate a brief warm-up routine which utilizes light flexibility and cardio-pulmonary exercises.

Cardiovascular and Conditioning

This is where the "work" is done. The heart rate will raise, blood flow increases within the working muscles, blood pressure rises in response, and the metabolic rate dramatically increases. Increased demand for oxygen causes participants to breathe more heavily, and the body will typically flush and break out in a sweat.

Movement
Participants will engage in different types and forms of movement throughout a fitness class. The pace and intensity will vary, but generally they will follow a bell curve pattern. Movement will start gradually (low impact in the warm-up phase), and then increase in both intensity and complexity during the conditioning portion, before a gradual decrease a movement is performed during the cool-down section of the class.

Equipment
The type of equipment used during a fitness class can vary greatly, and are often specific to the individual class. Step classes, for example, will use platforms. Pilates classes may use foam rollers or resistance bands. Most classes will use mats at the end for the final cool down and flexibility portions. Make sure to learn the rules and requirements, as well as the safety features, of any equipment incorporated in a class. Cycling classes will use bikes.

Cool-Down
The goal of the cool-down is to transition the body from vigorous activity back to a resting mode. Without a cool-down, blood may pool in the lower extremities, leading to dizziness and/or fainting. Think of the warm-up and cool-down as the bookends of an exercise routine; the cool-down will have the opposite effect of the warm up, decreasing the heart rate and the body temperature.

Flexibility
Controlled static stretching is an important piece of the cool-down. It's particularly important to incorporate flexibility into a cool-down, because the muscles are still warm from the conditioning part of the class, and therefore are more pliable.

Domain III: Progression and Modifications

Your certification will also require, in addition to your working knowledge of exercise and the human body, a comprehensive understanding of how to instruct your clients in a fitness setting. There are many components to a safe and successful learning environment—we'll review them here.

COMMUNICATION

Instruction—in fact, all types of effective interaction—depends strongly upon proper communication. Whether verbal or non-verbal, communication serves as the means by which we are able to interact with each other and exchange ideas. However simple this concept may seem, there are multiple variables which must be considered for effective communication. We'll cover these concepts more fully later; for now, we will go over those which apply particularly to Group Instruction.

Learning Types

A successful instructor, when deciding on a means of communication, must consider the audience. There are three main different types of learners: visual, auditory, and kinesthetic. By understanding the individual preferences of each type of learner, trainers can teach in a manner that helps participants successfully comprehend new concepts in an exercise class.

> **Visual Learners** benefit the most from visual aids. While they have no problem understanding verbal communication, they tend to retain and comprehend information more fully if they are given visual examples. Bring diagrams or incorporate posters when providing information to visual learners. If you are describing the best kinds of exercise gear to use, bring in equipment for demonstrations. Physical demonstrations of exercise techniques are also helpful in an instruction setting. Simple cues such as, "Watch yourself in the mirror," or "Follow along with this movement" serve visual learners very well.

> Demonstrations are also useful for **Kinesthetic Learners,** those who receive information best when it is incorporated with an action. This type of learning is also called **tactile.** Again, having visual aids which the client can touch will help them absorb information more fully. For example, bring in a replica of five pounds worth of fat. Have your client hold it to gauge its weight or see how it feels. In an exercise setting, have your client participate in the movements of an exercise before performing it independently. Draw the client's attention to how the correct movements *feel*.

> **Auditory Learners**, on the other hand, are the **listeners** of the bunch. They respond best when instructions are spoken or detailed. For example: If you provide a handout detailing the different levels of fitness, an auditory learner would benefit from hearing through each point and having the chance to ask for clarification.

You can identify your clients' learning preferences by watching for verbal and non-verbal clues during initial meetings and subsequent training sessions. For instance, clients who look closely at visual aids posted on workstations most likely have a dominant visual pathway and will require a demonstration of skills. Conversely, clients who listen intently to verbal instructions, but rarely refer to the visual aids, probably prefer auditory input. Kinesthetic learners typically understand an exercise fully only after having completed a set or two.

Verbal and Non-Verbal Communication Strategies

Once you've determined the best way in which your communication will be received, you can begin to incorporate a mixture of verbal and non-verbal communication strategies.

A good instructor uses both verbal and non-verbal cueing techniques. Each is important in facilitating an effective class. **Verbal** communication is exactly what it sounds like: using vocalizations to communicate ideas or directions. This can come in many forms: counting, cueing, feedback, etc., all of which we'll cover in later sections. However, verbal communication is more than just the words spoken.

Tone is an important aspect of verbal communication, and can change the meaning of a phrase drastically. You may have heard the saying, "It's not what you say, but the way you say it." This is very true! Don't believe us? Take a look at the following phrase:

I never said she needed more exercise.

That sentence can be read seven different ways, depending on which word you stress. And that's just emphasis! Tone also relies heavily on **attitude**. If you as the instructor sound bored, it doesn't matter if you are encouraging participants to engage in the exercise; they are likely to become bored as well.

Volume is another important aspect of verbal communication, and it should be considered particularly when using amplification equipment. If your microphone is too loud, the noise can be irritating or distracting for participants. Alternatively, lowered volume can lead to confusion and frustration.

While verbal communication is important and is usually considered the primary mode of communication, even more important is **non-verbal** communication. People can use words to say something different from how they truly feel, but body language rarely lies. In a fitness-instruction setting, you should be aware of the different non-verbal strategies you could use to enhance your communication.

Movements such as pointing and clapping can indicate upcoming movements, and your own posture— upright, alert, etc.—can affect the attitude of the class. When giving individual attention, respectful eye contact is essential to effectively delivering information.

During instruction, make sure to use universal terms and hand signals. Otherwise, no one will understand the cueing. Also, avoid using any gestures that might be confusing or construed as disrespectful.

Prevention of Vocal Stress

As an instructor, you may eventually teach several classes a week—sometimes several in one day. Doing so can put tremendous stress on your vocal cords. Using a microphone, in addition to using non-verbal cues, can help; but the following basic guidelines, as outlined by AFAA (Aerobics and Fitness Association of America) should also be observed:

- Stay in good health.

- Remain hydrated.

- Pace your vocalizations and allow for rest.

- Avoid medications; irritants like smoke, smog, etc.; and foods with irritating effects.

- Avoid negative vocal behaviors such as screaming, shouting, or talking loudly.

- Limit talking in noisy places.

- Support volume with breath from the diaphragm, rather than force from the vocal chords.

- Warm up your voice.

- Develop good breathing habits.

Teaching Styles

The manner in which an instructor or trainer teaches should be based not only on personal preference, but also upon the type of instruction that will provide the greatest benefit to class participants.

1. **Command**: When an instructor uses the command style, they cue (or **command**) every movement of the participants: pre-impact, impact, and post-impact. This style is often used to ensure that beginner-level participants can mimic movement.

    - **Advantages**: Direct and immediate relationship between command and response, making tasks progress quickly and correctly.

    - **Disadvantages**: Assumes that all participants can perform the tasks, when in reality a classroom will hold individuals of varying fitness levels. The instructor is also restricted from providing individual attention.

2. **Practice**: As the name suggests, this teaching style allows participants to practice a specific task (which has been demonstrated by the instructor) while making their own alterations according to nine factors: order of tasks, starting time per task, interval, pace and rhythm, stopping time per task, initiating questions for clarification, location, attire, and appearance and posture. During the period of practice, the instructor is able to observe and provide help/feedback as required.

    - **Advantages**: This style allows participants to proceed at their own proficiency level, while the instructor provides individual feedback. It is also helpful for learners who learn best under trial-and-error conditions.

    - **Disadvantages**: Some participants may not be able to perform the task without being guided or prompted throughout the entire maneuver. There could also be those who are either too challenged/not challenged enough by the task without being able to adjust the task independently.

3. **Reciprocal**: This style of teaching is ideal for situations demanding social interaction. Participants are divided into pairs: one observer and one doer. The pair are given a card which describes a task; the doer performs the task, while the observer provides instruction and feedback. The instructor is available to facilitate, answer questions, and provide further feedback.

    - **Advantages**: Both the doer and the observer benefit; the doer learns through performing the task, and the observer from observation.

    - **Disadvantages**: As the observer is not a certified professional, their instruction/feedback may not always be accurate.

4. **Self-Check**: Here, the instructor is less involved in the process. Participants are given criteria by which to check themselves as they work independently, also engaging in self-assessments. The instructor is available for questions, but leaves most of the direction to the participants.

   - **Advantages**: This style gives the student the opportunity to critique his/her own execution based on what they have learned. It is a good way to improve confidence and proficiency.

   - **Disadvantages**: As this is a very individual process, it is best used by advanced students rather than the novice. This style of teaching is not very practical with tasks which cannot be broken down into multiple steps.

5. **Inclusion**: This style allows participants to set their own level of challenge. The instructor provides multiple tasks with varying degrees of difficulty, and the participants can choose which degree they would like to complete first, and then progress as they choose.

   - **Advantages**: Allows for mass participation consisting of members of all fitness levels.

   - **Disadvantages**: Participants may incorrectly assess their capabilities, increasing the chance of injury or lack of challenge. Participants may also feel intimidated by those performing more challenging tasks than their own, and may become self-conscious.

6. **Discovery**: There are two style types of discovery: guided and divergent. In both, the instructor poses a question to the participant. In guided discovery, the instructor has a specific predetermined answer in mind, and their questions will purposefully lead the learner to this understanding. Divergent discovery, on the other hand, depends upon the participant/s to discover the correct answer on their own, as they come up with multiple answers to the posed question.

   - **Advantages**: Participants grow in confidence and motivation as they are forced to problem solve, which also increases retention of information.

   - **Disadvantages**: It may be time-consuming to wait for participants to discover the correct answer. Also, some participants may remain silent, opting to allow their peers to answer instead.

MONITORING

For most healthy people, the benefits of exercise far outweigh the risks. However, even for those populations which are healthy and active, potential risks still exist when engaging in physical activity. As a professional, you should understand the potential of those risks, the most common being:

1. **Overuse Injuries**: These occur when the body has been taxed beyond its capabilities. Remind your clients that being healthy and well means treating their bodies well; this includes exercising, of course, but also learning to realize when the body needs rest. Common overuse injuries are muscle pulls, sprains, and strains.

2. **Over-exertion**: These injuries are similar to overuse injuries in that both occur when the body has been pushed beyond its capabilities. Over-exertion may result in exhaustion, shortness of breath, dizziness, and other dangerous conditions.

3. **Accidents**: It is important to always pay close attention to clients in order to create the safest environment possible; however, you should always be prepared for the "human element" of physical exertion. These can include dropped equipment, improper form, inadequate spacing which results in collision between bodies, etc. – resulting in accidental injury.

4. **Prior Health Conditions and Injuries**: When a client has a history of injuries or health conditions, they are more likely to be at risk for future ones. It is important for you, as the professional, to be made aware of any and all existing conditions. There is nothing sneaky about finding out about existing conditions; simply ask before commencing a program. For example, you could say, "If anyone has any health conditions or injuries, let me know before we begin." You can even go around before beginning, if you have the time, and speak individually with each client, introducing yourself and ascertaining their individual fitness needs.

All of these risks, and those less-common, can be exacerbated by many factors, including:

- When the exercise is particularly vigorous, as in extreme or competitive sports.

- When training is occurring under adverse conditions, as in high altitudes, extremely hot or cold climates, or outside climates which consist of rocky or uneven ground.

- An existing history of health conditions (obesity, impaired glucose tolerance, elevated HDL, elevated blood pressure, and/or a family history of any of the above).

- Clients who drink or smoke.

Though uncommon, strenuous exercise can even result in sudden death in non-athletic, teenage, and young adult athletes with inherited cardiac disorders, as well as in older adults with risk factors for coronary heart disease.

Being an instructor carries a certain amount of responsibility – participants not only trust you to provide a high-quality program, but they will also look to you during emergency situations. Accidents always happen, and it's your responsibility to know how to recognize the signs and correct responses of potentially problematic situations.

Fatigue
Can be defined as a lack of energy and strength that could be characterized as exhaustion. The following are signs and symptoms of fatigue:

- Chronic tiredness or sleepiness.

- Sore or aching muscles.

- Poor concentration.

- Reduced ability to pay attention to the immediate situation.

- Slowed reflexes and responses.

- Impaired hand-to-eye coordination.

- Impaired decision-making and judgment.

- Headache.

- Dizziness.

- Muscle weakness.

- Appetite loss.

- Reduced immune system function.

- Blurry vision.

- Hallucinations.

Under Exertion
Though not so worrying as over exertion, you should also be able to identify when a participant isn't putting forth enough effort. That way, you can prompt for an increase in intensity as needed. Signs of under exertion might include a lack of interest, excuses, stall tactics, and be resistance to performing.

Over Exertion
The signs and symptoms of fatigue apply here as well, with the addition of pain in muscles, joints, lungs, or—in extreme situations—the chest.

- Dizziness.

- Acute shortness of breath or labored breathing.

- Sore and painful muscles.

- An alarmingly higher than normal exercise pulse.

- Irregular or rapid heartbeat.

- Nausea.

- Chest pain.

- Overheating and perspiring profusely.

- Pain in the lower abdomen.

- Blue lips and fingers.

- Lack of coordination.

Dehydration

Dehydration occurs when one's fluid intake drops below optimum levels to fuel normal biochemical and physiological functions. Signs and symptoms of dehydration include:

Mild Dehydration

- Feeling very hot and perspiring profusely.

- Irregular or fluttering heartbeat.

- Extreme shortness of breath or labored breathing.

- Nausea.

- Sore and painful muscles.

- Chest pain.

- An exercise pulse that is higher than recommended for your size and physical condition and does not slow after exercising has ended.

- Lack of coordination.

- Low abdominal pain.

- Dizziness/Unconsciousness.

- Blue lips and fingers.

Severe Dehydration

- Rapid pulse.

- Vomiting.

- Muscle spasms.

- Painful urination with very low urine volume.

- Dim vision or temporary blindness.

- Chest pain.

- Confusion.

- Respiratory depression.

- Neuromuscular seizures.

- Unconsciousness.

Some of the more common medical conditions are cardiopulmonary and metabolic conditions, such as diabetes, hyperglycemia, hypoglycemia, and cardiac arrhythmias.

Diabetes

As discussed, diabetes is one of the leading causes of death in the United States, and those with diabetes can experience serious complications during physical activity. Exercise is often prescribed to prevent and control diabetes; however, those with diabetes can experience serious complications during physical activity.

Diabetes' full name is **diabetes mellitus**, which defines a group of diseases which alter how the body uses blood glucose (blood sugar). Glucose is an important source of energy for the body, fueling cells which make up muscles and tissues, providing the fuel for metabolism, and acting as the primary source of fuel for the brain.

There are two types of diabetes:

- **Type 1** diabetes (insulin dependent diabetes) typically occurs in people under the age of 40 and is a chronic condition in which the pancreas produces little or no insulin.

- **Type 2** diabetes (insulin resistant) occurs when the body becomes resistant to the effects of insulin or fails to produce enough insulin. This is the more common form of diabetes.

It is important to learn if any of your clients have either type of diabetes. However, be aware that many people may not wish to share personal conditions for some personal reason. Stress the importance of learning these details and offer several means for your clients to communicate this information with you privately, via email, phone, or office consultations.

Once you become aware of a client with diabetes, you should provide and make sure clients follow these general safety guidelines:

- Know the ideal blood glucose level. (Between 100 – 200mg/dL, one to two hours after eating.)

- Regulate glucose levels by timing workout sessions in relation to meals and insulin dosage.

- Check blood glucose levels before and after workouts.

- Clients should consult their physicians regarding the possibility of reducing insulin by 10% – 50% when beginning an exercise program, due to pronounced effect which exercise has on insulin production.
- Perform a proper warm-up and cool-down.

- Wear appropriate footwear.

- Remain hydrated.

- Avoid exercising in extreme conditions.

Hyperglycemia

Diabetes is not the only condition which effects blood glucose. **Hyperglycemia** means that a person has high blood glucose. ("Hyper" means "high," or "above.") Since the ideal blood glucose level is between 100 and 200 mg/dL; a hyperglycemic body will have a glucose level that exceeds 200 mg/dL.

Some people constantly have high blood glucose, and they should inform you of this condition. However, hyperglycemia can occur in healthy populations as well, due to a sudden change in diet or body composition. In either case, both you and your clients should be aware of the symptoms and treatments of hyperglycemia.

Symptoms associated with hyperglycemia:

- Headache.

- Increased thirst.

- Frequent urination.

- Blurred vision.

- Fatigue.

- Cardiac arrhythmia.

- Deep and rapid breathing.

If you notice any of these symptoms and suspect that a client has become hyperglycemic, you should:

1. Give the client water.

2. If possible, have the client test his or her blood sugar levels.

3. If necessary, have the client take the level of insulin prescribed by his or her doctor. If the client does not have an insulin prescription, seek medical attention immediately.

Hypoglycemia

On the other side of the spectrum is **hypoglycemia**, which means low blood glucose, specifically a glucose level below 70 mg/dL. (A good way to remember the difference between "hyper" and "hypo" is through rhyming: "hypo" rhymes with "low.")

Symptoms associated with hypoglycemia:
- Headache.

- Dizziness.

- Sweating.

- Hunger.

- Shakiness.

- Anxiety or nervousness.

- Irritability or moodiness.

99

- Confusion.
- Pallid skin.

Just as with hyperglycemia, even healthy populations ought to be aware of the possibilities of becoming hypoglycemic.

If a client shows symptoms of hypoglycemia, health fitness professionals should:

1. Stop the workout.

2. Have the client sit or lie down.

3. The client should check his or her glucose levels if possible.

4. Raise the blood glucose levels immediately with a rapidly absorbing carbohydrate such as a piece of candy or fruit juice. *Avoid diet soft drinks, as they have no sugar.*

5. If the client has a glucose gel or tablet, he or she can take this instead of a carbohydrate.

6. Insist the client rest until signs of improvement occur.

7. Check the client's blood glucose levels at signs of improvement in condition.

8. A blood glucose level of 100 mg/dL is acceptable to resume activity.

9. If the client shows little to no signs of improvement, seek medical attention immediately.

Cardiac Arrhythmias: Cardiopulmonary Conditions
Cardiac arrhythmias, or heart rhythm abnormalities, happen when the heart does not pump properly, which causes it to beat too fast or too slow. Though most arrhythmias are harmless and may be reduced by regular exercise, serious problems can sometimes occur during physical activity.

Bradycardia
Bradycardia is a condition wherein the heart has an abnormally slow heart rate, which is less than 60 beats per minute. This can result in the following symptoms:
- Fainting.
- Dizziness.
- Lightheadedness.
- Fatigue.
- Shortness of breath.
- Angina.
- Confusion.
- Tiring quickly during exercise.

If a client shows symptoms of bradycardia, health fitness professionals should:

1. Stop the workout.

2. Perform CPR, if needed.

3. Seek medical attention immediately.

Tachycardia

Bradycardia has an opposite condition: tachycardia. **Tachycardia** is when the heart has an abnormally *fast* rate, exceeding 100 beats per minute. Tachycardia may produce no symptoms, but extreme cases can lead to unconsciousness, stroke, and sudden cardiac arrest. These are serious, dangerous conditions, and you should be aware of the following symptoms:

- Dizziness.

- Lightheadedness.

- Palpitations.

- Angina.

- Shortness of breath.

If a client shows symptoms of tachycardia, health fitness professionals should:

1. Stop the workout.

2. Perform CPR, if needed.

3. Seek medical attention immediately.

Self-Monitoring in the Participant

When people know the range of intensity that they should be training in, they can improve their conditioning and measure their progress while ensuring that they stay in a safe training zone. A practical way for participants to measure or gauge their exercise intensity is by paying attention to how they feel at any given time during the workout.

It is important for all participants to monitor how they are feeling during the workout, but it becomes particularly important for people with hypertension, pregnant women, and older participants. By monitoring their intensity levels, high-risk participants can avoid potentially dangerous outcomes.

Heart Rate

Heart rate monitors can be used, but traditionally a manual check of the radial artery or the carotid artery is done. The radial artery is the ideal site at which to check one's pulse. It is done by using one hand to locate the pulse on the thumb side of the opposite wrist. While holding the hand palm facing up, the index and middle fingers are used to touch the artery and feel the pulse.

Talk Test

The Talk Test is a subjective scale that tests whether or not a participant is able to count or speak in short sentences. It is best used in conjunction with a heart rate and RPE test (see below). Note that this test may not be appropriate for students who are well conditioned or during interval training.

Borg's Ratings of Perceived Exertion (RPE)

The Rate of Perceived Exertion should be used as a general guide that encourages clients to pay close attention to the physiological responses to exercise that their body experiences. Most facilities will post RPE charts in aerobics studios for participants to reference, and instructors should explain this chart during the class.

Rating of Perceived Exertion (RPE)	Breathing	Percentage of Heart Rate (HR)
0	Normal	Resting HR
1	Light increase in breathing; able to converse	Slightly above resting HR
2		
3	Notable increase but still comfortable	50%
4	Heavier breathing; harder to maintain conversation	65 – 70%
5		
6	Even heavier breathing; able to converse but do not want to do so	70 – 80%
7		
8	Difficulty breathing; unable to hold conversation at all	80 – 90%
9		
10	Very labored breathing	100%

Dyspnea Scale

Dyspnea refers to shortness of breath or difficulty breathing. This scale, while subjective, is helpful for those who suffer pulmonary conditions like asthma. Participants rate their ability to breathe using the following scale:

+1	Mild and noticeable difficulty to the participant but not others.
+2	Mild and some difficulty, noticeable to others.
+3	Moderate difficulty, but participant can continue exercising.
+4	Severe difficulty, and the participant must stop exercising.

Metabolic Equivalent of Tasks (METs)

The MET indicates the cost of a physical activity in energy, expressing it as a multiple of the resting metabolic rate. Essentially, the MET is a unit that estimates the amount of oxygen used by the body during exercise.

> 1 MET = The energy (oxygen) consumed by the body when it is at rest (for example, sitting quietly or reading a book).

The more a person exerts him- or herself during an activity, the more oxygen must be consumed; thus, the higher the MET level.

Activities burning three to six METS are considered *moderately intense*. Activities burning over six METs are generally considered *vigorously intense.*

Zone Training

To calculate training zone, use this formula:

HRR (heart rate reserve) * Intensity % + RHR (resting heart rate)

To calculate HRR, subtract the Resting Heart Rate from the Maximum Heart Rate (as determined by a test) or Estimated Maximum Heart Rate (determined by subtracting age in years from 220). THR or training zone can be determined from the HRR.

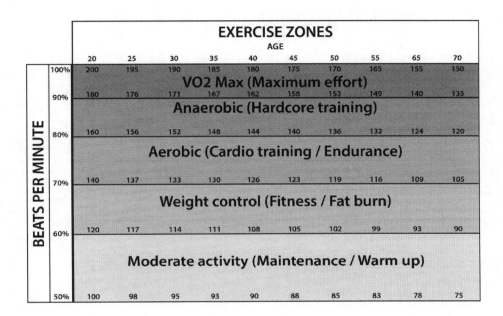

Note that many factors can affect a person's morning pulse and training pulse. Stress (work, emotional, etc.) will increase the heart rate. Nutrition, especially hydration levels and caffeine, will also greatly influence the heart rate. Medication (like beta blockers) can slow OR increase the heart rate. Until the body adapts (usually after a week or so) heat and altitude will increase heart rate.

Heart Rate Specifics

During Warm-Up
The heart is at fifty to sixty percent of its maximum rate. This is the most comfortable training zone and is best for those new to exercise or seeking to prepare the body for more vigorous activity. This zone has been shown to help decrease body fat, blood pressure, and cholesterol. It also decreases the risk of degenerative diseases and has a low risk of injury.

During the Cardiovascular Phase
The heart is at sixty to seventy percent of its maximum rate. This phase is also known as the fat burning zone. Those with an average fitness level are generally comfortable working out at this level for an extended period of time. Studies have revealed that by working out in this zone, muscle mass is gained, heart health improves, and the body can be trained to burn fat more efficiently.

Muscular Conditioning

The heart is at seventy to eighty-five percent of its maximum rate. During resistance training the heart rate is disproportionately elevated, relative to oxygen consumption. Heart rates are much higher for resistance training than for aerobic conditioning. Significant gains will be made by training in this zone, specifically in endurance. Half of all calories burned in this zone come from fat.

Cool-Down

The heart is at fifty to sixty percent of its maximum rate. Much like the warm up, cool-down is a comfortable training range that is used to bring the body back to a normal state of activity. As body temperature and heart rate decreases, so too does the heart rate.

Applications and Limitations in the Calculations of Target Heart Rate

Traditional target heart rate measurements generally have wide application and can provide a good read for most individuals. However, there are some limitations.

> **Age-Predicted Maximum Heart Rate**: It was discovered in 2001 that this equation underestimates HR max in older adults, risking underestimating physical stress during exercise, and resulting in incorrect levels of intensity in prescribed exercise programs.

> **Percent of Heart-Rate Reserve**: Percent HRR accurately predicts percent of maximal oxygen consumption in diabetics. It may also effectively monitor exercise intensity, regardless of the presence of diabetes. While the RPE scale is also valid, it is a slightly less accurate monitor of exercise intensity in diabetic individuals.

> **Measured Maximum Heart Rate**: The MMHR formula is not exactly accurate for everyone. American sports scientists have modified the basic formula to allow for gender: $214 - (0.8 * age)$ for men, and $209 - (0.9 * age)$ for women. However, to get a true reading, a person must really work up their heart rate. Therefore, without the ability to increase heart rate it may not be possible to get an absolute number for maximum heart rate.

PROGRESSION

Variety, Progression, and Modification

No matter how fine-tuned and effective an exercise program may be, eventually participants will require modifications and variety. Exercisers face a particular challenge in sticking with a fitness program. Let's face it, sometimes working out can get stale, becoming too "routine." How many times have you heard people express their reluctance to work out as, "It just starts to feel like a chore"?

This factor, coupled with the many other road blocks exercisers deal with, can cause clients to give up their efforts. That's where you, as the instructor/trainer, come in. Your knowledge and motivation are often critical to the student's success.

Variety

Infusing variety into workouts is beneficial for the participant, but also for the instructors. Professionals often have to deal with boredom too, after all! Challenge yourself by varying your classes through the regular introduction of new choreography, more progressions into higher intensity levels, various modification options during class, etc. Even something as simple as moving a class to a park or playground can boost morale and enthusiasm. Changing the music is a quick way to change the mood of a class. The addition of new equipment is another fun way to change things up and create a new challenge.

Variety can be found in a wide number of factors in a class, including:

- Class location.
- Difficulty level.
- Introduction of new/more complex choreography.
- Music selection.
- Type of equipment used.
- Increased modification options.
- "Challenge" classes (a class that lasts ninety minutes instead of the usual sixty, for example).

Progression

Progression should be one of the primary goals in any fitness program. If workouts are not progressive, results will stagnate or even regress very quickly. During the duration of an exercise program, clients will begin to see improved stamina, strength, and balance. In order to continue to see gains, however, workouts must adjust to become more challenging.

Once the body adapts to a program, an occurrence often referred to as "plateauing," you can affect one or more of the following components: intensity, frequency, and duration.

> Say you have a client who initially could not run a mile inside of fifteen minutes. Eventually, over the course of their exercise program, the client gains the strength and stamina to run one mile a week comfortably within ten minutes. What are your options to progress your client's fitness forward?

> You may choose to increase the **intensity** – in this instance, have your client run at a faster pace. Or, you could increase **duration**. Since in this example time spent exercising is a dependent variable, duration can be increased by having the client run two miles, instead of one. Finally, you may have chosen to increase **frequency**, having your client progress to running a mile twice a week or more.

Remember, communication is key. If your client is not comfortable with any modifications, then work with her to create a program which will still allow her to move forward. Consider the following concepts of progression, regression, and modification when creating your programs.

The **Principle of Progression** suggests that in order to continue to see physiological gains, a particular level of overload must occur within an optimal time frame. Progressing a client too quickly can cause injury; too slowly, and boredom can set in to preclude results. Rest and recovery are also essential components of progression. The pace at which one progresses depends on functional capacity, medical and health status, age, and individual activity preferences and goals. A generally healthy adult can increase endurance in three stages of progression: initial, improvement, and maintenance.

The **initial phase** is the starting point for the client and will vary by individual. In this phase, it is important to determine a comfortable endurance and cardiovascular challenge. The initial phase will typically last four to six weeks, but the time frame can vary by individual.

Clients will then move into the **improvement phase**, wherein noticeable changes in stamina and strength are realized. While this phase will last longer than the first, usually four to six months, the progression moves at a much faster pace. Intensity, for example, will be rapidly progressed because the client will be training at a target range of fifty to eighty-five percent of the maximum heart rate. Duration may also be increased. It is important to reemphasize that the type of progression and time frame for progression is highly variable and depends on the individual.

Maintenance begins once a client has been exercising for six months. A reassessment is helpful at this point, as initial goals have been achieved and new ones need to be formulated. A maintenance program should be designed that will help the client to stay at his current level of fitness and keep him engaged over time.

On the other side of the spectrum from progression lies **regression**, which means going back to the most basic form of an exercise. For example, instead of having a client perform a single leg squat, have her do a basic squat to engage both legs. It can also mean reducing the load or the intensity of exercise. This concept of "getting back to basics" is often misconstrued as counterproductive, boring, and even as a sign of failure. After all, if a person has been bench pressing 120 pounds and is switched to a program that only calls for 100 pounds, the exercise could seem too easy and even useless.

There are many instances when it is appropriate to regress a training program.

- Stress or Fatigue: If a client is experiencing stress or fatigue from a previous workout or from the rigors of everyday life, it is a good idea to modify the normal training program. Pushing the client through a tough training session may be counterproductive. Remember, exercise by its very nature puts stress on the body—even seemingly simple exercises have their effects. However, if the body is not allowed to rest and recover, improvements will be hindered.

- Inability to Perform: Sometimes unfair assumptions are made regarding an individual's fitness level. For instance, a client able to deadlift 100 pounds may struggle to do a single leg squat. A client who can run a mile in six minutes may have difficulty swimming twenty laps. If a client is not able to perform an exercise in a safe and effective manner that will benefit him, a modification should be provided.

- Reaching a Plateau: At some point in a training program, most people will not be able to progress further without changing things up. For example, if a client has reached her maximum lifting weight, you cannot ask her to lift more weight. Instead, the trainer should introduce new equipment to have the client work her muscles from different angles, producing a new challenge.

An exercise can be regressed in any number of ways, the most common of which being a decrease in the load. In addition, load length and impact can be decreased, and the entire exercise can be modified altogether to work the muscle from a different angle.

Modification is often necessary to help a client learn to perform an exercise. Other times, a client cannot perform certain aspects of an exercise and therefore requires modifications. For instance, a client who cannot perform a plank can modify the movement by resting on the elbows instead of fully extending the arms.

Accommodating Various Fitness Levels

Skill levels vary dramatically from person to person. Observation is critical to identifying the needs and limitations of each participant. Noticing things like how quickly people pick up on choreography, how quickly they move, how well they work their coordination, do they modify movement on their own, etc. all provide insight into what limitations may exist in the class.

It also helps to just ask! At the beginning of the class, ask if you have anyone new to the particular activity. Make yourself available—and let people know that you're available—before or after class to answer any questions; some instructors even allow two minutes before class solely to answer any questions that participants may have.

The key to creating multi-level classes that meet the different levels of ability are modifications. We've provided some examples of modifications for the following components of a program; take some time and think of your own, as well.

Flexibility
Show modifications that account for a limited range of motion. Specifically ask if any participants have injuries or discomforts before exercising, and create modifications that limit stress on those areas. Have equipment on-hand that will help with such modifications, like chairs or yoga blocks.

Exercise
Prepare multiple options for different exercise moves, and pay attention to see if the majority of the class is able to follow along. If participants are unable to follow along after the exercise has been broken down, then select a less complex exercise in order to keep the class moving.

Balance
Have at least three different options for balance exercises, and demonstrate each. Keep a careful eye on participants to make sure they are performing the maneuvers correctly. Have equipment on-hand that will help with modifications. You can encourage participants to steady themselves on walls or chairs. You could also have equipment to increase intensity, such as stability balls.

Teaching Strategies

1. **Identifying Areas of Weakness**: The instructor should construct a class that safely addresses any weaknesses that participants have. Observing how participants move and how they respond to exercise, choreography, the use of equipment, and the type of music will help the instructor to identify any such weaknesses.

2. **Designing Exercises and Movements**: The exercises and movements done should be appropriate for the skill level of the class. For instance, in an advanced step class, participants will expect faster music, advanced choreography, and greater intensity. It is the instructor's obligation to meet those expectations.

3. **Slow-to-fast**: The instructor teaches complicated moves at a slower rhythm before performing them at a faster pace. Once the participants can perform the movements correctly, they can perform the movements at tempo (on beat on the music). This manner of teaching can be time-consuming, and the heart rate will drop when moves are done at a slower pace. Therefore, such instruction is best performed early in the class.

4. **Repetition Reduction**: Instructors often perform several repetitions in an effort to show participants the move. Often participants need to see a movement or a pattern of movements done repeatedly to grasp it. Once the majority of participants can perform the move, the number of repetitions can be reduced.

5. **Spatial**: The instructor uses this teaching method when introducing new body positions. Distinguishing body-alignment cues are explained to participants prior to attempting the exercise. An example of a spatial clue would "lengthen through the spine."

6. **Part-to-whole**: The instructor teaches a skill in smaller segments. Each segment is practiced and perfected before the next segment is introduced. This is repeated until the entire movement has been taught. Instructors will cue this by saying "adding-on."

7. **Simple-to-Complex**: This method helps instructors teach at multiple skill levels. In this method, movements start simple before becoming more complex. Sequences are then modified slightly so that participants have movement options. The participant must choose which is appropriate for their skill level.

SPECIAL CONSIDERATIONS

Special Populations are persons with diseases and/or other metabolic conditions. Usually, these persons are under the care of a physician, or some other health care personnel. Examples would be pregnant women, the elderly, those at risk for diseases such as diabetes, and those with medical problems such as cardiac patients. Other common conditions include asthma and arthritis.

Pregnant women must understand that even though they may have been active prior to pregnancy, their body is undergoing severe changes and will respond differently to exercise during pregnancy. Of course, physical health is also extremely important for both the mother and the baby, and so a pregnant client may very likely come to you for advice on appropriate exercises. Keep the following guidelines in mind.

- Pregnant woman need to avoid potentially harmful activities such as: extreme sports, activities that have a high risk of falling, jarring exercises, and jumping exercises.

- An elevated blood pressure can sometimes cause spotting, or even induce labor, within pregnant women.
    - Unless otherwise cleared by a physician, have pregnant women avoid extreme exercise that would excessively raise their blood pressure, or put strain on their spine.

- Hydration, hydration, hydration! Even when not exercising, the demands of the baby require pregnant women to consume much more water than usual. Pay attention to your client – if they say they are thirsty, stop immediately for a water break.
  - Having a pregnant client break often for water both ensures that they are getting adequate hydration, and keeps their body temperature at a safe level.

- For pregnant clients, low-impact activities are best. Recommend walking, water aerobics, or gentle yoga.

Seniors face two areas of major concern as they age: weakening bones and muscles. Exercise can have a profound effect on these two conditions. Low-impact cardiovascular activity and resistance training are most beneficial to seniors. Doing so in moderation and following proper exercise progression is the key to staying fit as a senior.

Chronic Diseases

Chronic diseases such as diabetes, cancer, cardiovascular disease, chronic heart failure, and pulmonary disease are the leading cause of mortality in the world. They are diseases of long duration, and are generally slow in progression. Chronic diseases do not resolve spontaneously and are rarely cured completely. They are the most common and costly of all health problems, but they are also the most preventable.

Cardiovascular Disease (CVD)
Any disease affecting the heart or blood vessels is considered CVD. CVD increases the risk of sudden death, heart failure, heart attack, stroke, cardiac rhythm problems, and high blood pressure; CVD therefore decreases quality of life and life expectancy.

Cardiovascular disease may be caused by structural abnormalities, infection, inflammation, environmental responses, and/or genetics; above all, those living an unhealthy lifestyle are susceptible. Adopting a healthy lifestyle by exercising, practicing healthy nutrition (especially limiting fatty foods), avoiding or quitting smoking, and minimizing stress will help prevent CVD.

Many risk factors for CVD are preventable or treatable. They include: excess weight, smoking, excessive alcohol consumption, physical inactivity, illegal drug use, high cholesterol, high blood pressure, diabetes, and stress. Other risks include having had a previous heart attack, having a family member who has heart disease, increasing age, gender, and race.

Atherosclerosis (plaque formation) refers to the amount of lipid (fat) deposits in the medium and large arteries of the body. With a sedentary lifestyle, a diet that involves a high intake of saturated fat, high blood pressure, smoking, and any other toxic agent to the body, the endothelial cells of the artery can become damaged. Lipoproteins are deposited at the damaged site of the artery, and plaque formation (atherosclerosis) begins. These deposits can eventually impede blood flow through the artery. Atherosclerosis can occur anywhere in the body; but when it occurs in the coronary (heart) arteries, it can increase risk for a heart attack.

Exercise training is an ordinary treatment for cardiovascular disease today because of the known health benefits of conditioning and strengthening the heart. Exercise, or aerobic training, improves blood circulation in the heart, as well as oxygen delivery. Exercise training reduces body fat and blood pressure; lowers total cholesterol, triglycerides, and LDL (bad cholesterol); and increases HDL (good cholesterol).

The level of exercise in which a client first engages will vary with each individual's needs and abilities. However, it is important for you as a professional to always stress the importance of physical activity to prevent CVD.

Obesity

Obesity has been labeled a chronic disease by the Centers of Disease Control (CDC), and it has become a major health concern for people of all ages: one in every three adults, and nearly one in every five young people aged six through nineteen are obese. This chronic disease is one of the leading causes of Type II diabetes, heart disease, and stroke. Obesity, however, can be preventable.

Modifiable behaviors to combat obesity include getting a sufficient amount of physical activity every day and consuming a healthy diet that is rich in lean proteins, high in fruit and vegetables, and low in saturated fats. When lack of activity and a high intake of saturated fat cause an overweight body, a person is at a higher risk for cardiovascular disease.

Diabetes

Diabetes is characterized by **hyperglycemia** (elevated blood sugars). There are two common forms of diabetes: Type I and Type II.

> **Type I** diabetes is an autoimmune disease wherein the insulin-producing beta cells of the pancreas are destroyed by the own body. The pancreas cannot produce insulin, making it necessary for the person to administer insulin for the rest of their life. Type I diabetes is treatable, and maintainable, but not preventable.

> In **Type II** diabetes, insulin receptors become resistant to insulin, and blood glucose cannot readily move into the cells. This causes hyperglycemia. Diabetes, if not controlled, can increase the risk for many complications that affect the blood vessels and nerves, including vision impairment, kidney disease, peripheral vascular disease, atherosclerosis, and hypertension. Type II diabetes can be prevented.

Developing some of these complications increases the risk for heart disease and stroke. Many people with Type II diabetes are relatively inactive and overweight (or even obese). The development of excessive abdominal fat can also be attributed to age, family history, and lifestyle choices. In today's society, with its growing obesity epidemic, Type II diabetes is rapidly developing in children. However, it can be managed like obesity—by consuming healthy foods and maintaining a healthy diet.

Physical Impairments

Visual impairments affect some millions of people in the United States, ranging from near-sightedness to total blindness. Some people are born with visual impairments; others attain them due to injury to the eyes, injury to the brain, or simply the aging process. Such people may wear corrective eyes glasses, or contact lenses—in those cases, having the client be mindful of such jarring activities such as jumping or running can help prevent the loss or damage of such property.

- Depth perception may be affected—space the client accordingly so as to minimize the risk of injury to themselves or others.

- When demonstrating techniques, be aware that those with visual impairments may not be able to see you very well. As such, narrate your actions. Instead of saying, "Do this," while demonstrating a punch, instruct the client to "keep wrists straight and aligned with the shoulder. Don't overextend or lock the elbows."

Hearing impairments—such as noise-induced hearing loss (NIHL), which refers to damage to hearing caused by loud noises—are quite common. Hearing loss can also occur due to head trauma, ear infections, pregnancy complications, and genetic disorders. Hearing aids are often helpful in restoring at least partial hearing loss. Avoid high-pitched musical cues, as those with impairments/aids often have difficulty hearing such sounds. Environments over 75 dB are considered dangerous to everyone, not just those with hearing impairments, so always be mindful of your sound equipment settings.

According to the Census Bureau there are 32.5 million people in the US living with **severe disabilities**, physical impairments caused by injuries of the skeletal system along with the muscles, joints, and ligaments. Such disabilities include amputations and disabilities due to spinal cord injuries (SCI). Severe SCI can result in partial or complete paralysis. In these cases, consult thoroughly with your client's physician in order to determine safe and appropriate means of exercise.

The Importance of Exercise

Exercise provides many benefits to bodies with and without impairments. Although exercise will not always prevent or cure chronic diseases, it should still be encouraged. Exercise improves insulin sensitivity and reduces disease. Exercise protects against coronary artery disease, dyslipidemia (high cholesterol), hypertension, and obesity.

It can sometimes be difficult to exercise around impairments, but there are always options. Both you and your client need open communication with the client's physician. You need to be sure your client is medically stable before prescribing exercise.

Human Growth and Development
Human development is the process of growing to maturity. From a biological standpoint, human development is a continuum, starting with fertilization before going on to prenatal development, birth, and then further growth to adulthood. The age groups are as follows:

- Infancy: 3 weeks to 1 year.
- Childhood: 1 to 10 years.

- Juvenile: 10 to 16 years.

- Adolescence: 16 years to early 20s.

- Adulthood: Early 20s to 64 years.

- Senescence: 65 to 100 years and older.

A person's age must be considered when designing and implementing any type of structured exercise program.

Diseases: Factors and Treatments

In order to maximize the effectiveness of medical and surgical management, having a solid understanding of a variety of chronic diseases is essential. Knowing the risk factors and treatments for the following conditions helps health fitness professionals, at all levels, to prevent, diagnose, manage, and treat with competence.

Chronic Obstructive Pulmonary Disease (COPD) is a group of lung diseases that block airflow as you exhale. Individuals with COPD experience shortness of breath, or **dyspnea**, due to this difficulty in exhaling all the air out from their lungs. The main conditions are:

1. Emphysema: A condition that damages the alveoli by destroying the inner walls and making them weaker and less elastic. This reduces the surface area for oxygen exchange.

2. Chronic asthmatic bronchitis: Chronic inflammation and narrowing of the airways leading to the lungs, causing coughing and wheezing.

3. Asthma: A chronic breathing disorder characterized by frequent bronchospasms.

4. Cystic Fibrosis: In most cases, the symptoms of COPD do not appear until there is significant lung damage and continue to worsen over time. Symptoms include shortness of breath, wheezing, chest tightness, and chronic coughing. COPD is a leading cause of death and disability, with the most common cause being smoking. Age and occupational exposure to dust and chemicals are also key risk factors.

If COPD is suspected, the following tests may be used for diagnosis:

- Chest X-ray.

- Computerized Tomography (CT).

- Arterial blood gas analysis: Measures how well your lungs are bringing oxygen into your blood and removing carbon dioxide.

- Sputum examination: Analysis of the cells found in mucus helps to rule out lung cancer or a bacterial infection.

- Pulmonary Function Test (PFT): A post bronchodilator ration of FEV1 (forced expiratory volume in 1 second) / FVC (forced vital capacity) of ≤ 0.7 is indicative of nonreversible airflow limitation.

Since the damage is irreversible, treatments focus on controlling symptoms and minimizing damage to improve quality of life. Quitting smoking is an essential step in the treatment plan as it is the only way to stop COPD from progressing.

Medications, such as bronchodilators, inhaled steroids, and antibiotics are used to assist in symptom relief.

Other forms of therapy include supplemental oxygen and pulmonary rehabilitation. There are also surgical treatments for individuals with severe emphysema:

- Lung volume reduction surgery: a small wedge of damaged lung tissue is removed. This creates extra space in the chest cavity for the remaining lung tissue and diaphragm to work more efficiently.

- Lung transplant.

Restrictive Lung Disease is a group of lung diseases characterized by restriction in the lungs causing the inability to fully inhale. This results from conditions causing stiffness in the lungs, the chest wall, weak muscles, or nerve damage. These conditions include:

- Interstitial lung disease/Pulmonary Fibrosis: A group of lung diseases affecting the interstitium (the tissue and space around the air sacs of the lungs).

- Sarcoidosis: A disease that results from a specific type of inflammation of tissues of the body. It can appear in almost any body organ, but it starts most often in the lungs or lymph nodes.

- Obesity: Excessive body fat.

- Scoliosis: An abnormal curvature of the lumbar spine.

- Muscular Dystrophy or Amyotrophic Lateral Sclerosis (ALS): A group of inherited disorders that involve muscle weakness and loss of muscle tissue.

Restrictive Lung Diseases restrict and reduce lung volume and tidal volume due to one, or all of the following: loss of functioning of the alveoli-capillary unit, altered mechanical function of the thorax and pulmonary system, or secondary cardiovascular dysfunction. The same diagnostic tests that are used to diagnose COPD are used to diagnose restrictive lung diseases, too; according to the National Institute of Health, the following treatments can also be utilized:

- Immunosuppressant drugs (*Imuran, Cytoxan, Rheumatrex, Trexall*): These keep your immune system from attacking and destroying healthy tissue. They also can be used to slow or stop the growth of abnormal tissue or cells.

- Corticosteroids (inhaled or oral): These can reduce swelling and inflammation and suppress the immune system so it doesn't attack healthy cells.

- Anti-inflammatory drugs: Reducing inflammation and swelling can ease symptoms.

- Anti-fibrotic drugs: These investigational drugs may slow or stop extra tissue from forming on the lungs.

Individuals diagnosed with either intrinsic (internal causes) or extrinsic (external causes) restrictive lung disease can also benefit from oxygen therapy and pulmonary rehabilitation.

Cardiovascular Disease (CVD) refers to any disease that affects the cardiovascular system, especially cardiac disease, vascular diseases of the brain and kidney, and peripheral arterial disease.

According to the American College of Sports Medicine and the American College of Cardiology, there are multiple non-modifiable and modifiable risk factors for the development of cardiovascular disease.

Non-modifiable Risk Factors: Advancing age, gender, and family history.

Modifiable Risk Factors: Tobacco smoking, dyslipidemia, hypertension, physical inactivity, overweight/obesity, diabetes (Type II), and metabolic syndrome.

Diabetes: Diabetes refers to a spectrum of metabolic diseases. The diabetic suffers from high blood sugar because the pancreas fails to produce enough insulin to metabolize sugars (Type I or IDDM), or because the insulin that is produced does not affect the cells (Type II or NIDDM). The risk factors for diabetes depend on disease etiology. Family history is the major risk factor for developing Type I diabetes; risks are especially high for those with a parent or sibling with the disease.

Type I diabetes may also be caused by injury or diseases of the pancreas, inhibiting its ability to produce insulin; a range of relatively rare infections and illnesses can cause it as well. Risk factors for Type II diabetes include:

- Obesity/Overweight.
- Ethnicity.
- Insulin resistance.
- Hypertension.
- Family History.
- Sedentary Lifestyle.
- Age.

Even with recent breakthroughs and advancements in science and technology, there is currently no cure for diabetes. Keeping the level of glucose in the blood within the normal range, however, can control it. Patients with Type I diabetes can be treated with insulin several times a day, while patients with Type II diabetes may not need insulin.

Diabetes in these patients is typically controlled with diet and physical activity, as well as oral hypoglycemic agents such as *Metformin, Glucophage*, and *Glucotrol*. In cases where glucose levels are not well controlled with oral glycemics, some Type II patients find that they do need to be placed on insulin therapy.

Edema is caused by fluid trapped in the body's tissues, generally seen in the feet, ankles, and legs; however it may appear in the face, hands, abdomen, and elsewhere. Signs and symptoms include:

- Tissue swelling under the skin.

- Shiny or stretched skin.

- Skin that displays "pitting": when it is pressed, an imprint remains on the surface.

- Swelling in the abdomen.

Significant risk factors for edema include congestive heart failure, liver, kidney, lung, and thyroid diseases; these can exacerbate edema, too, as can some medications that treat diabetes, blood pressure, and pain. Furthermore, edema may be caused by poor nutrition, trauma, severe inflammation, allergic reactions, burns, and clotting.

Depending on its cause, edema can be temporary or permanent. For instance, edema caused by lung diseases may be alleviated by quitting smoking. Patients suffering from chronic heart failure may benefit from treatment for coronary artery disease, weight management, monitoring fluid and salt intake, and limiting alcohol consumption.

Metabolic Syndrome

Metabolic syndrome is characterized by a group of metabolic risk factors, including the following:

1. Central Obesity: Excessive abdominal body fat (adipose tissue); this may be measured by waist circumference. In men, a waist circumference greater than forty inches indicates obesity while in women it is indicated by a waist circumference greater than thirty-five inches.

2. Atherogenic Dyslipidemia: High triglycerides, low high-density lipid (HDL) cholesterol, and other blood fat disorders that allow build-up of plaque in the artery walls. Blood HDL levels are indicated by triglyceride levels greater than or equal to 150mg/dL (at fasting). For men, artherogenic dyslipidemia is indicated by triglyceride levels of less than 40mg/dL, indicating low HDL cholesterol, while for women the disease is indicated by triglyceride levels of less than 50mg/dL.

3. Insulin Resistance/Glucose Intolerance: This disorder appears when the body is not able to properly use insulin or metabolize glucose at a fasting blood glucose level greater than or equal to 110mg/dL. Most individuals with metabolic syndrome display insulin resistance as it often accompanies other metabolic risk factors. Glucose intolerance is another emerging risk factor and often appears in patients with longstanding insulin resistance.

4. Proinflammatory State: A proinflammatory state is indicated by increased high-sensitivity C-reactive protein (CRP) levels in the blood. This can be caused by obesity, because inflammatory cytokines released by adipose tissue may increase CRP levels.

5. Prothrombic State: A prothrombic state is indicated by high levels of fibrinogen or plasminogen activator inhibitor [-1] in the blood. Fibrinogen, like CRP, is an acute-phase reactant; it increases in response to a high-cytokine state.

6. Hypertension: Hypertension is indicated by increased blood pressure (130/85mmHg or higher) and is usually accompanied by obesity and insulin resistance; it may, however, stem from multiple causes.

Effects of Exercise on Pulmonary Disorders

Exercise can benefit even those who suffer from permanent pulmonary disorders, for pulmonary disabilities result from the side effects of those disorders, which are generally treatable. While pulmonary rehabilitation does not cause major changes in the degree of chronic obstructive pulmonary disease (COPD) or in airway obstruction, patients do become able to walk farther and limit dyspnea as their muscles become more conditioned and they adapt to better pacing.

Impairments like anxiety, depression, poor nutrition, weakness, and dysfunction of peripheral and respiratory muscles are treatable; furthermore, health-related quality of life measures (QOL) and dyspnea (both overall and exertional) respond to treatment as well. Patients' maximal exercise capacity is found to increase during exercise testing. Finally, exercise reduces the risk of coronary artery disease (CAD) in those with pulmonary disorders, as the two diseases are generally associated.

Effects of Exercise on Asthma
The bronchial narrowing characteristic of asthma is triggered when exercise introduces a large volume of air deep into the lungs. Usually, the nose, mouth, and throat warm and moisturize air entering the lungs so that the air is at the same temperature as the bronchial tubes themselves once it enters the chest. However, during moderate or vigorous exercise, as breathing rate increases, the time and ability to warm and humidify incoming air decreases. Asthma results as the bronchial tubes contract and cause coughing and wheezing in response to the loss of heat and moisture as cold air enters the lungs.

There are a few ways to prevent exercise-induced asthma. During a cold day, cover the nose and mouth with a scarf in order to trap warm and moist air. Serious athletes should also engage in a light warm-up before competition to reduce risk of symptoms. In addition, taking inhaled medications ten minutes before exercise such as a prescribed beta-agonist bronchodilator like *albuterol* can prevent asthma symptoms.

Effects of Exercise on the Metabolic Syndrome
The Metabolic Syndrome is the collection of central obesity, dyslipidemia, insulin sensitivity, hypertension, and impaired glucose tolerance. Metabolic Syndrome will soon become primary risk factor for chronic disease states, including heart disease, in the United States, overtaking cigarette smoking. Maintaining a healthy diet and regular use of proper medication will address specific risk factors; however, all forms of physical activity impact the components of Metabolic Syndrome as discussed below:

1. Hypertension. There is a significant amount of evidence that aerobic training helps to reduce blood pressure and SBP.

2. Dyslipidemia. Low saturated fat diets combined with exercise lower total cholesterol, LDL-C, and triglyceride concentrations, while increasing HDL-C levels. Alternatively, nutritional supplements combined with exercise, decreased total cholesterol, LDL-C, and triglyceride concentrations, while increasing HDL-C levels. Combinations of lifestyle therapies, including exercise, are effective in improving cholesterol levels.

3. Glucose Intolerance/Insulin Insensitivity. Both acute and longer periods of exercise benefit insulin sensitivity. After even a single exercise session, short-term effects appear. These are mainly mediated by the metabolic changes in insulin signaling inside the muscle tissue.

   As the intracellular accumulation of intermediary metabolites interfering with insulin signaling decreases, related modifications in fatty acid metabolism strongly impact improved muscle insulin sensitivity. Chronic exercise leads to improved glucose tolerance.

4. Obesity. To treat obesity, it is essential to exercise, yet reduced exercise tolerance is a hallmark of this disease. As a result, very obese patients cannot engage in beneficial exercises, so treatment must include both dietary restriction and exercise. The severely obese should prioritize dietary treatment, while the mildly obese should prioritize exercise. Exercise is also essential for obesity prevention.

Effects of Exercise on Diabetes

Type I Diabetes (Insulin Dependent) disrupts the body's ability to metabolize fuels like sugars, starches, fats, and proteins, thereby disrupting normal energy metabolism both during activity and at rest.

The pancreas releases insulin, a hormone, into the blood after digestion. Insulin permits carbohydrates, which are absorbed as glucose, and proteins to enter muscle cells. The muscle cells either store them or use them for energy. Those with Type I diabetes cannot produce the insulin necessary for this process to take place. As a result, glucose builds up in the blood as it cannot enter the cells.

People with Type I diabetes require daily insulin injections in order to stabilize glucose at levels as close to normal as possible, making these individuals insulin-dependent. Type I diabetics must regulate their blood glucose (blood sugar) levels to avoid complications.

If glucose levels remain unchecked for extended periods, people with Type I diabetes run the risk of developing heart disease, kidney failure, blindness, and nerve dysfunction.

Exercise effectively controls blood sugar levels because it uses glucose as fuel. Having an insulin-like effect on glucose, exercise enhances its uptake into cells and counteracts the elevated blood glucose levels that manifest after eating. Those with type 1 diabetes who exercise may require smaller or fewer injections of insulin.

Type II Diabetes (Non-insulin Dependent) occurs when insulin does not remove glucose from the bloodstream. By interacting with body cell mechanisms, insulin usually facilitates the passage of glucose from the blood and into tissues; however impairment of this process, called insulin resistance, leads to hyperglycemia, Type II diabetes, and other health problems.

Following a single episode of exercise, insulin can more easily clear glucose from circulation for twelve to forty-eight hours. Regular exercise makes this effect more sustainable, minimizing hyperglycemic consequences over time. As the skeletal muscles adapt to physical training, glucose control improves as well because those muscles use glucose for energy.

The harder muscles work, the more glucose they need. Regular activity increases the body's capacity to store glucose, causes new blood vessels to develop within muscles, and improves the ability of insulin to move glucose into cells.

Effects of Exercise on Coronary Artery Disease

The mechanisms responsible for a decrease in coronary artery disease vary and include:

1. The effects of exercise on CAD risk factors:

   - Decrease in resting and exercise blood pressures.

   - Decrease in total cholesterol, LDL cholesterol, and triglyceride levels.

   - Increase in HDL cholesterol.

   - Improved glucose tolerance and insulin sensitivity.

   - Decrease in body fat percentage and waist circumference.

2. A reduction in cardiac oxygen demand at rest and at submaximal workloads, leading to an increase in ischemic/angina thresholds.

3. A reduction in platelet aggregation.

4. An improvement in endothelial function and tone.

The following classes of medications are frequently used in the treatment of CAD; therefore, knowing how they respond to exercise is crucial when performing diagnostic tests and prescribing exercise therapy.

1. **Angiotensin-Converting Enzyme (ACE) inhibitors**: Used to treat hypertension, these act by reducing myocardial oxygen demand through reducing vascular resistance. They may increase exercise tolerance in those with left ventricular dysfunction and reduce resting and exercising blood pressure. Examples: *Atacand, Avapro, Cozaar, Micardis, Diovan, Benicar.*

2. **Beta Adrenergic Blockers:** Used to treat hypertension, left ventricular dysfunction, and angina, these reduce ischemia by decreasing oxygen demand and control ventricular dysrhythmias. They reduce resting and exercising heart rates and blood pressures and may increase exercise tolerance in those with ventricular dysfunction. Examples: *Toprol, Tenormin, Corgard, Inderal*

3. **Calcium Channel Antagonists**: Used to treat hypertension, angina, atrial fibrillation and supraventricular tachycardia, these reduce ischemia by altering the determinants of oxygen supply and demand. They reduce resting and exercising blood pressures; some may reduce resting and exercising heart rates. Examples: *Cardizem, Calan, Calan SR, Covera HS, Verelan PM.*

4. **Nitrates:** Used to treat angina and as a vasodilator in heart failure, these reduce ischemia by decreasing oxygen demand and by allowing a small increase in oxygen supply and decrease resting and exercising blood pressures. They are available in short and long-lasting forms. Examples: *Imdur, Nitrostat, Nitroquick, Nitrobid.*

5. **Digitalis:** Used for congestive heart failure, this enhances myocardial contractility, increasing stroke volume, and blunt SA and AV node conduction, reducing resting and exercising heart rates in those with tachycardia and atrial fibrillation. Example: *Digitalis.*

6. **Diuretics:** Used for mild hypertension, these reduce blood pressure by increasing renal secretion of sodium and potassium, resulting in a loss of water in the urine, mildly affecting resting and exercising blood pressures. They may increase exercise tolerance in patients with congestive heart failure. There are several types:
    *   Thiazides: *Hydrochlorothiazide, Indapamide.*
    *   Loop: *Bumex, Lasix.*
    *   Potassium-sparing: *Midamor.*
    *   Aldosterone receptor blockers: *Inspra, Aldactone.*
    *   Combination diuretics: *Moduretic, Maxzide.*

Domain IV: Professional Conduct, Safety, and Risk Management

PROVIDING FEEDBACK

Instructions and observations aren't the only things that need to be communicated to your participants. Throughout the review, we've mentioned the importance of feedback, an important way to let clients know they have your attention. More importantly, specific positive feedback is an effective tool for keeping clients motivated during the initial stages of change.

There are three types of feedback:

Corrective Feedback
Your client is performing crunches, and you notice that he is lifting from his neck, rather than his core. Here, you would apply **corrective feedback** to inform him of the proper way to execute the movement. Corrective feedback is sometimes called **negative feedback**, because it addresses errors. However, avoid the phrase "negative feedback," as it (understandably) brings to mind negative connotations.

This feedback should focus on the effectiveness (or ineffectiveness) of the strategy employed, not on the individual. Instead, place emphasis on the assessment of the strategy used, the outcomes, and the need to use a more effective strategy. Remember, the *strategy* was unsuccessful, not the individual. Using examples also helps in corrective feedback; people tend to respond more favorably.

Positive Feedback
Even when a person does not make mistakes, it is important to provide feedback in order to keep her engaged, motivated, and happy with her progress. Positive feedback emphasizes what was done well, and encourages it. It's wise to always include positive feedback, even with corrective feedback, in order to avoid discouraging and frustrating your client.

Value Statements
Value statements are not based on fact; rather, they are positive or negative judgments based on how the person making the assessment interprets or perceives a situation. For example, you may judge an exercise regimen to be extremely helpful to a client's goals. However, this type of feedback is subjective, and therefore best to avoid. The client may not share the same opinions, after all.

Neutral Statements
Neutral statements are more difficult to make than you'd think. They communicate only facts, and include zero opinions. An example of a neutral statement might be "Jim completed fifty pushups in one minute." No reference has been made as to whether or not Jim did the pushups well. Only the observable facts are conveyed. It takes a little more effort to erase all types of feedback. Even phrases such as "well done" fall outside the realm of neutrality. Stick to the facts

Components of Effective Feedback

Informational Rather than Controlling
Feedback should build a person up, not tear her or him down—nor should it have a controlling effect on an individual. The best feedback provides relevant, factual information that can be used for improvements.

If, after receiving feedback, a person feels beaten down or forced to make changes, then that feedback was not effective. Your language can have a huge effect on feedback. Imagine that you have a client who needs to correct her posture. Which feedback sounds better?

"Straighten your back."

"Make sure your back is straight."

"Watch your back; is it straight?"

If you chose the last option, then you're correct! With this feedback, you've completely removed your own control from the situation. The second option is good for this reason as well. Direct commands, such as the first option, ought to be avoided until you've established rapport with your client.

Based on Performance Standards
Feedback based upon performance standards is **actionable** feedback. The receiver knows exactly where he stands, especially with regards to his goals. For example: "You're five repetitions short of twenty! You're close to your goal." Or, "You made it through the entire class without needing to stop! Now you can increase your difficulty." This feedback is not diluted with unnecessary information or opinions.

Specific and Immediate
Giving specific feedback in the moment is ideal. Don't wait until the end of the entire session to address a point from the beginning. Immediate feedback gives the receiver the opportunity to reference recent behavior and make any necessary changes. In all feedback, remain specific. Ambiguity won't help the receiver at all: she may continue to make the same mistake again and again, without knowing exactly what it is she is meant to do. For example, use "Keep your elbows in and your guard up," rather than "Watch your elbows."

Correcting Movement

After providing feedback, you should attempt to help correct any issues found. For instance, your client performs an overhead squat and their arms fall forward. This is likely an indication that the *latissimus dorsi, teres major*, and *pectoralis major/minor* are overactive and the *mid/lower trapezius, rhomboids,* and *rotator cuff* are underactive. You should prescribe exercises that would strengthen the underactive muscles to correct the imbalance. Such exercises might include bent or seated rows and external rotation with resistance tubing. These exercises would progress over time as the client's strength increases.

Yet how do you apply effective instructional methods for improvement? Focus on three things: exercise techniques, balance, and movement.

Exercise Techniques
Prevention and rehabilitation programs are essential in correcting imbalances and alignment, as well as improving range of motion issues. Should you encounter such issues, then you can create a program which consists of exercises emphasizing multi-planar movements through the full muscle action spectrum. Examples would include performing crunches on a stability ball or doing single leg squats on a BOSU. Such exercises will isolate and challenge muscles that are deconditioned.

Balance

Balance is measured by an individual's ability to maintain center of mass over base of support. It is imperative for daily function, rehabilitation, performance training, and injury prevention.

Good balance requires both mobility and stability. Training should be designed to continually challenge one's equilibrium using controlled instability. For instance, a client may start with doing a single leg squat on a floor. Once this is no longer difficult, the client can progress to performing the single leg squat on a half foam disc. This is a **systematic progression** that will take the client's balance to its optimum level.

Movement

Corrective techniques will improve body function and movement over time. Systematic and progressive training will alleviate imbalances and compensations while increasing range of motion. Eventually, muscles will begin to fire equally; ultimately restoring balance to the body. For many people, corrective exercises not only help to improve mobility, but also reduce and/or eliminate pain.

Using Touch

Touch is a powerful medium and is an integral part of how we communicate. Fitness professionals regularly utilize touch in their jobs every day through spotting, stretching, or correcting body alignment. Yoga instructors in particular touch clients in an effort to help them adjust their form and to execute poses accurately.

However, it is important to remember that those in the fitness industry have an obligation to maintain a professional distance when working with all participants. You must set the appropriate boundaries in a working relationship with your clients.

The following are guidelines for using touch:

1. **Ask First**: Phrases such as, "Can I correct your posture?" or "Will you let me move your arm to where it needs to be?" Will avoid startling your client and, most importantly, will make sure that they are comfortable with the contact. If clients seem uncomfortable, anxious, or upset—even if they say yes—then do not touch them.

2. **Gauge Necessity**: Do not touch participants unless it is absolutely necessary to the instruction or their safety.

3. **Explain**: Even if you know why contact may be necessary, your client may not. Explain the need for touch in each situation, and be prepared to use an alternate method of instruction if your client disagrees.

4. **Watch Your Client**: If touching makes the participant feel uneasy, do not persist.

5. **Be as Impersonal as Possible**: Use the back of your hand, instead of your palm, to facilitate touch. This makes the contact both less personal and less potentially invasive.

6. **Use Good Judgment**: It should go without saying, but always be aware of the situation and the consequences of all actions.

Certain types of feedback can work as reinforcement tools, such as extrinsic and intrinsic rewards. **Extrinsic rewards** are tangible items such as free t-shirts or training sessions after clients complete an established goal.

These extrinsic rewards work well in the early stages, but trainers need to help clients realize **intrinsic rewards** for prolonged success. Intrinsic rewards are the benefits that come when clients attain a higher level of fitness. The improved health and wellness at this point serve as the rewards that inspire permanent success.

CREATING A SAFE ENVIRONMENT

Classes taught in community environments like churches or recreation centers are often not as well-equipped as gyms of fitness studios. If working out on a carpeted floor, avoid highly complex choreography to protect joints and prevent falls.

Outdoor workouts can be exhilarating and fun. The instructor, however, has less control over the environment and should take extra steps to keep the participants' safety in the forefront. Scope out the area before the workout to observe things like traffic flow and noise level. Make sure the area is clean and clear of debris or uneven surfaces like rocks. It is also wise to check the weather beforehand or have a contingency plan for inclement weather.

Some trainers and instructors work with clients in their homes. If doing so, explain to the client how much open space the workout will require. Ask about pets and children. Make sure that water and a towel are on hand. Again, it may be wise to set up a meeting prior to the first workout to inspect the space and be sure that it is suitable for the workout.

Exercise environments can be varied and individualized to a high degree, yet there remain precautions and recommendations that ought to be considered across the board.

Altitude

Exercising in a **high altitude** environment affects breathing rate, which can decrease the amount of oxygen into and out of the lungs. An increase in altitude decreases the partial pressure of oxygen and reduces the amount of oxygen bound to hemoglobin (the protein in the blood that carries oxygen). As a result, the volume of oxygen carried in each liter of blood decreases. If exercising in a new environment at a different altitude, allow time for adjustment, usually a day or so, before beginning activity more strenuous than easy walking.

Changes in Temperature—Heat

When someone is exercising in **hot conditions**, extra stress is placed on the body; add that external heat to the increased core body temperature, and a person can risk serious illness when exercising in the heat. To cool one's body, the heart beats faster—and harder—to pump blood to the surface of the skin. It does this in order to assist with sweating, which is the body's attempt to cool itself. However, this leaves less blood for the muscles, and since the body utilizes the muscles during exercise, the heart again works harder to provide the necessary blood. Also, if **humidity** is high, the body faces added stress, because sweat doesn't readily evaporate from skin, pushing one's body temperature even higher.

Whenever temperatures reach seventy degrees Fahrenheit and the humidity is seventy percent or higher, the heart must work harder to cool the body. When the outdoor temperature climbs into the eighties (Fahrenheit) or beyond and there is high humidity, then the risk to health also rises.

If the body cannot cool itself enough, the heart experiences a high level of strain, leading to heat sicknesses. **Heat exhaustion** is a form of heat sickness that can lead to heat stroke. Symptoms of heat exhaustion include:

- Heavy sweating with cool, or clammy, skin.

- Fatigue.

- Nausea.

- Fainting.

If a person suffering from heat exhaustion is not quickly relieved, he or she may suffer from organ damage, or **heat stroke**–a potentially fatal condition.

Everyone is susceptible to heat stroke; however, those afflicted with heart disease and other cardiovascular diseases are more vulnerable because the heart may not be able to perform the necessary extra work to maintain a cooler body temperature.

Some heart conditions require medications that reduce water in the bloodstream, thereby limiting the body's power to cool itself off in a hot environment. Clients taking beta-blockers or diuretics should work with their doctor to determine the proper amount of water to drink in hot temperatures in order to prevent heat stroke.

Other medications decrease cardiac output, or the amount of blood pumped by the heart, which in turn decreases blood flow to the skin. Consequently the body's ability to sweat and cool itself is hindered. Other medicines decrease the amount of blood pumped by the heart (cardiac output) and limit blood flow to the skin, so the body is less able to cool itself by sweating. Some related medicines affect the sensation of thirst or increase the body's production of heat. Take extra precautions when designing exercise programs for clients with heart conditions and/or those who take medications that alter their heart rate.

Finally, heat stroke is an emergency. The following symptoms indicate heat stroke; if a client displays them, immediately apply cool water to the client's skin and seek medical assistance.

Symptoms of Heat Stroke:

- Hot, dry skin without sweating.

- Pounding pulse.

- Dizziness.

- Nausea and/or vomiting.

- Confusion.

- High fever.

- Unconsciousness.

If a client has heart disease, it is especially critical that they are told to avoid exercising when the temperature and the humidity are both high. In those cases, recommend that the client delay any intense exercise until the temperature has dropped and the humidity has reduced. Avoid exercising during the hottest part of the day (early mornings are ideal). Dress in loose, light-colored clothes that will reflect sunlight; use sunscreen; and stay hydrated. Hi-tech performance fabrics work well for wicking away perspiration. Also consider prescribing physician-approved exercises unaffected by the weather such as indoor exercises or swimming.

Changes in Temperature—Cold

On the other end of the spectrum, exercising in **cold conditions** can cause hypothermia: a decrease in body temperature wherein heat loss exceeds heat production and the body's temperature falls below normal. As temperatures drop, the heart exerts more effort to maintain the body's core temperature; this exertion stresses the heart, increasing the risk of heart failure.

In addition, cold weather may affect hormones, cause blood vessel constriction, or trigger other effects in the body that increase the risk of a heart attack or heart failure. Therefore, people with heart disease and babies and young children with complex congenital heart conditions are at risk in very cold environments.

Regardless of their cardiovascular conditions, clients should wear layers, including hats and gloves, when exercising outdoors. Advise clients to work slowly when engaging in physically taxing work like shoveling snow. Emphasize these warnings in particular to clients known to have cardiovascular diseases. Finally, clients should discuss exposure to cold weather during outdoor activities with their doctors, and they should determine which activities are safe to perform.

Hypothermia and Heart Attack Symptoms

The following are symptoms of hypothermia and heart attack. If you or your client notice these symptoms and suspect either of these medical emergencies, **dial 9-1-1 and seek medical attention immediately**.

Symptoms of Hypothermia:

- Shivering.

- Confusion.

- Fumbling hands.

- Fatigue, drowsiness or exhaustion.

- Memory loss.

- Slurred speech.

Symptoms of Heart Attack:

- Pain or discomfort in one or both arms, the neck, jaw, back, or stomach.

- Discomfort in the chest (not necessarily chest pain.)

- Breaking out in a cold sweat.

- Feeling nauseous or lightheaded.

- Shortness of breath (may be accompanied by chest discomfort).

When exercising in cold temperatures, dress in layers, taking care to protect the hands, feet, and ears. Avoid cold, rainy weather and days wherein the wind chill is extreme. Wear footwear that will provide sure footing, and stay hydrated.

Nutritional Requirements

Water should be consumed before, during, and after exercise. This will help avoid dehydration while regulating the body's core temperature. Drink about sixteen ounces of water two hours before exercise. Sports drinks with sodium and carbohydrates (but limited sugar) may be beneficial if exercising in a hot, humid environment for over an hour.

Food fuels the body, enabling activity. The ideal pre-exercise meal is low in fat and fiber, contains moderate amounts of carbohydrates and protein, and is high in fluids. Avoid unfamiliar foods or those difficult to digest, and stay clear of fried food and soft drinks.

Time	What to Eat
Two to Three Hours Before Exercise	300 – 400 Calories: Mix of carbohydrates, proteins, and fat.
One to Two Hours Before Exercise	200 Calories or Less: A snack consisting mostly of carbohydrates and a small amount of protein.
Fifteen Minutes or Less Before Exercise	Very light snack. A handful or raisins or crackers totaling about twenty-five grams would be ideal.
After the Workout (Preferably Within Forty-Five Minutes after Working Out)	At least ten percent of the meal should be proteins, and the rest a healthy balance of carbohydrates and fat to replace glycogen. If drinking a shake, avoid overly-sugary smoothies.

One of the most effective means of dietary assessments can be food journals. While many balk at the idea of recording everything that they eat, it is often an eye-opening exercise. Have clients evaluate dietary habits for three to seven days in order to become more aware of what they consume and when. However, it is important not to become obsessive. Clients should make small changes over time that can be easily incorporated into their daily routines to ensure long-lasting changes.

CLIENT INTERACTION

Rapport

The best trainers and instructors are those who can develop a positive relationship with people from all social, economic, and ethnic walks of life. Being approachable, friendly, and a good listener all play a part in building a bond with class participants. A few simple, yet effective, methods for developing rapport with class participants include:

- Learning Participant Names: Even though instructors teach many participants on a daily basis, it is a good practice to learn as many names as possible. This is an easy way to establish friendly relationships and establish adherence.

- Being Accessible and Approachable: Good instructors make themselves available to their participants. Arrive to class early so that you can greet and chat with students. If possible, stay a few minutes afterwards as well so that students can voice concerns, offer feedback, ask questions, or just say "thank you."

- Using Culturally-Appropriate Non-verbal Techniques: Non-verbals are powerful communication tools. A friendly image can be conveyed by using gestures like smiling, winking, making eye contact, nodding, opening palms, using open body position (avoid crossing arms), using the thumbs up sign, etc.

Interpersonal Communication Techniques to Enhance Rapport

Instructors and trainers should strive to develop effective communication skills that will aid them in building professional relationships. While building rapport can take time, it is a worthwhile investment.

The following are examples of effective interpersonal communication techniques:

- Active Listening: The process of being 100% focused and listening while someone else speaks, paraphrasing and reflecting back what is said without judgment or offering advice. For example, repeating what was stated shows good listening skills.

- Open-ended Questioning: Open-ended questions solicit additional information from the speaker because the question avoids a yes or no response. An example would be, "How can I help you?"

- Acknowledgement: Briefly summarizing what was heard and showing appreciation and understanding for the speaker is a good way to foster trust.

- Use of Empathy and Compassion: Empathy and compassion can go a long way toward effective relationship building. By showing empathy and compassion when problems arise, essential solutions can be developed and conflict can be avoided or diffused. These qualities are essential for handling complaints and retaining class participants.

Collaborative Goal Setting

Setting realistic goals to achieve an outcome is essential. Goals help people to focus, prioritize, follow-through, and measure progress. Collaborative goal setting is the process in which the fitness professional and the client come together in establishing goals and creating the road map to achieving them. The fitness professional plays a critical role helping clients understand their own visions for themselves, setting realistic expectations, creating effective action plans, and providing encouragement throughout the process. This type of collaboration spells success for those truly committed to the process.

Differences

Cultural, ethnic, and personal differences can influence communication, lifestyle, dietary habits, and personal and interpersonal behaviors. Working with people from different countries, diverse ethnic backgrounds, and with various personalities is both challenging and enriching. There can be language barriers, cultural ignorance, and general misconceptions. Fitness professionals must understand their client's needs despite such challenges. Doing so requires empathy, sincere interest, and earnest inquiry to overcome differences and remove barriers to success.

Concepts of fitness and exercise in the U.S. are different than in other parts of the world. For example, Americans tend to live more sedentary lifestyles and spend more hours at work than people in many other countries. A report published in 2010 in the American College of Sports Medicine's journal *Medicine & Science in Sports & Exercise* revealed that Americans spend far less time walking than people from other countries. Researchers used pedometers to monitor the steps of 1,136 Americans, and found that they averaged 5,117 steps a day, roughly two and a half miles.

Meanwhile, Australians averaged 9,695 steps a day, the Swiss averaged 9,650, and the Japanese took 7,168 steps daily. Many Americans realize the need to be more physically active and tend to rely more on going to gyms or participating in recreational and group exercise programs. Therefore, it is quite possible to work with a client from another country who may not understand the benefits of weight training, yet he or she may already be in good cardiovascular health from walking eight to ten miles a day. It is important to understand the lifestyle habits of fitness clients, whether they be cultural or ethnic in nature.

Helping clients from different backgrounds adopt better nutrition habits poses yet another challenge. Dietary habits vary tremendously from person to person. When cultural, ethnic, and even demographic differences are added to the mix, assisting clients to make better choices can be tough. While instructors and trainers may have a solid understanding of proper nutrition, they must learn to communicate such knowledge to clients who have very different dietary preferences.

It is wise for fitness professionals to avoid stereotypes and assumptions. Ask appropriate questions to gain a thorough understanding of the client. Use examples, demonstrations, and gestures if needed to communicate more effectively. Show respect for differences by inquiring about them and even studying up on them if it will help improve the relationship. Trainers and instructors should expand their knowledge and incorporate different training techniques, music, and ways of communicating to create a welcoming environment for each client.

Adherence

Starting and maintaining an exercise program can be a challenging, yet rewarding, endeavor. Over half of those who start an exercise program stop within the first six months. Adherence can be defined as one's ability to stick with an exercise program. The exercise program can be prescribed by a doctor or a trainer, or it could be a program that the individual has decided to adopt on his or her own.

Adherence can only achieved by choice. A person must make a conscious effort every day to exercise in order to reap the benefits. No one else can do that for them. Adherence to an exercise program is not easy. Most people face a great deal of obstacles and roadblocks that can derail them from sticking with a program. Those variables can include: lack of time, injuries, exercise boredom, lack of experience, cultural values, physical education level, peer or spousal support, and personal commitment.

It is the fitness instructor or trainer's job to guide people toward adhering to an exercise program, and ultimately, achieving their fitness goals. To improve adherence, it is important to understand what motivates each participant or client. Is she a novice trying out Zumba for the first time? Perhaps he is an avid cyclist looking for an off-season activity. They could be regulars who take two to three classes a week. Each participant has different motivations and the instructor must identify these distinct motivations in order to better serve each participant.

Methods for Improving Adherence

1. **Advanced Participants**: For these highly motivated, very fit individuals who exercise almost daily, it is important to keep them stimulated with a high-energy style of teaching that offers a sufficient challenge. It is also important to educate them on the potential risks of overtraining. Advanced participants often need help finding balance in their exercise programs. Encourage them to cross-train for maximum physiological benefit, increased challenge, and to avoid boredom.

2. **Consistent & Moderate Participants**: These participants are motivated by the satisfaction they derive from living a healthy lifestyle. Their primary goal is to get a good, safe workout most days a week. Exercise is their primary reward, and they typically require simple recognition such as a high five to recognize their persistent efforts.

3. **Novice Participants**: The newcomers need to feel welcomed and often require more attention. Ask them a few questions to better understand why they are taking the class. Inquire about their fitness background, and find out about any injuries they may have. Explain the class structure. Positioning the newcomer in the front of the class will give them a better view and allow the instructor to keep a better eye on them. Offer them assistance as needed. Also, increase the use of verbal and non-verbal cues to ensure that they are able to follow along. Finally, be positive and encouraging to the novice participant.

Adjusting Program Variables (sets, reps, intensity, rest periods, tempo) to Maximize Adherence
Because each participant has his or her own agenda, the instructor is challenged with the task of balancing everyone's needs. This is best done by providing options and modifications to all, and then catering to those individuals in need of the most assistance.

1. The **advanced participant** will seek the greater challenge, and having experience, will know how to achieve the desired intensity level.

2. The **consistent and moderate participant** is more focused on a good and safe workout and generally seeks a moderate workout.

3. Watch out for **novice participants**, as they in particular will rely upon your expertise to make adjustments. Since they are new to exercise, novices may try to push themselves beyond their capabilities. This type of behavior quickly leads to burn out. Therefore, a well-trained instructor will observe, anticipate, and facilitate the necessary adjustments. Appropriate adjustments may include fewer sets or repetitions, lighter weights, lower impact, greater or more rest periods, and a reduced tempo. Careful observation of each participant will ensure that everyone gets a safe and effective workout.

How to Establish an Atmosphere of Trust
Establishing an atmosphere of trust is best done by being professional, courteous, and sincere. Taking a genuine interest in class participants is crucial. Respect participants' time, get to know them, thank them, and be accessible. Your goal is to create a fun and safe environment for working out—who wouldn't want to come back to that?

Participant Treatment
While some participants may at times require more attention than others, it is imperative to treat everyone fairly and with equal attention. Remember that each participant is important and they each deserve the same level of professionalism and quality of instruction. Doing so will ensure a welcoming environment for everyone.

Factors That Create a Positive Experience for Class Participants

- Starting and ending class on time.

- Remembering participants' names.

- Having an appropriate music selection.

- Creating a clean, safe, and welcoming environment.

- Providing quality instruction.

- Being personable and accessible.

- Offering encouragement and inspiration.

On the other side of the spectrum, certain behaviors can create a negative experience for your participants. Obviously, these should be avoided.

Factors That Create a Negative Experience

- Being tardy and unprepared.

- Utilizing inappropriate music (i.e. containing profanity).

- Wearing unprofessional attire.

- Providing poor instruction.

Factors that Influence Program Participation and Adherence

1. **Biological Factors**: Many people who most need exercise face biological obstacles—such as obesity, disease, etc.—that may thwart their exercise ambitions.

2. **Psychological Factors**: The beliefs and expectations that people have regarding exercise can have a profound effect on their adherence to a program. If one believes that they will lose twenty pounds in six weeks, a fairly difficult goal, they may grow frustrated when they don't see their desired results.

   Other psychological factors to consider include the client's attitude towards exercise. For some, physical fitness may seem like a chore; or perhaps they find fitness facilities—full of healthy, active people—to be intimidating. Learning these factors, and modifying your program accordingly, is part of your job in creating a comfortable exercise experience for your client.

3. **Physiological Factors**: Physiological factors such as discomfort or muscle fatigue often cause people to abandon exercise efforts. The instructor can recommend a training regimen that allows more time for rest and recovery. Also consider recommending restorative activities like walking and yoga.

4. **Social Factors**: Self-esteem and efficacy, anorexia, bulimia, etc. are all factors that could possibly affect one's ability to stick with an exercise program. Self-esteem issues may cause an individual to avoid public settings such as a fitness class. Body image issues tend to have a similar effect. In such cases, encouragement is necessary, along with a class format that the participant would feel less self-conscious taking.

How to Identify Barriers to Exercise, Healthy Dietary Choices, and Weight Management

Just because a person signs up for fitness classes or joins the local gym does not mean he is ready to make lasting lifestyle changes. He may still be grappling with bad habits like fast food consumption and inactivity. As fitness professionals, we know that being fully committed to the change process is necessary for lasting success. Assessing a person's willingness to commit, however, can be complicated.

Asking appropriate lifestyle questions is an excellent place to start. Well-designed questions can help determine where a client is at on the ready-for-change scale. Include questions regarding alcohol and tobacco use, high blood pressure, sleep, relaxation, physical fitness, stress and anxiety, relationships, life satisfaction, and injuries. A sample questionnaire may include:

> Stress and Anxiety – Mark all that apply:
> _____ It is easy for me to relax.
> _____ I am able to handle stressful situations better than most people I know.
> _____ I do not have difficulty sleeping or staying asleep.
> _____ I hardly ever feel tense or anxious.
> _____ I am always able to complete the tasks that I start.

Try out this hypothetical. Think first about what you would do, and then check it against our direction.

> *A participant is having difficulty managing external factors, such as time and cost, which are affecting their adherence.*
> *What advice could you offer?*

Common external factors that get in the way of adherence are lack of time, lack of interest, and lack of resources. Instructors can offer abbreviated classes (instead of sixty minutes, thirty or forty-five minutes) at a higher intensity level; or teach clients how to incorporate more exercise into their daily routine. (Suggestions might include conducting walking meetings at work, walking during a lunch break, or waking up fifteen minutes earlier to do yoga stretches.)

Many people know that they should be more active, but they simply have no interest in gyms or fitness activities. Assessing the client's interests is key in this situation. Discover what she enjoys, and help her find enjoyable activities suitable for her. For instance, a client who likes to dance would likely enjoy a Zumba class and be more likely to stick with it. On the other hand, a client who is looking for variety might get more from a boot camp class that includes an array of activities.

Gym memberships are great, but may be financially out of reach for some. In such cases, outdoor workouts are a great option. Parks and trails provide an excellent backdrop for great cardio workouts. Even a school playground can be utilized for workouts. Instructors might also recommend YouTube channels of reputable, certified trainers. Subscribers can view quality at-home workouts free of charge.

DOCUMENTATION

ACE Guidelines

The American Council on Exercise has a very strong reputation. An ACE certification shows an individual's high standard of professionalism and knowledge in the field of health and fitness. As such, compliance with ACE Guidelines is absolutely necessary. Should an individual break any of these guidelines, the **Disciplinary Procedure** will be engaged. Causes for discipline include working despite being ineligible for certification; any irregularity as regards examinations (such as cheating); misuse of proprietary ACE materials; misrepresentation to ACE; professional misconduct and/or negligence; criminal activity; and failure to meet the requirements for certification or recertification.

To ensure fairness, ACE uses a three-tiered disciplinary review process consisting of review, hearing and appeals.

Please refer to the American Council on Exercise for full details.

Confidentiality

Maintaining and protecting a client's confidentiality is a must in the fitness industry. Professionals are often privy to sensitive information such as health history, current injuries, and/or medical issues—sometimes even very personal emotional struggles relative to body image and other concerns. Additionally, it is fairly normal to have access to a client's financial information including credit card and checking account numbers. As previously discussed, protecting confidentiality is not only the right thing to do out of respect for the individual, but it is also the law.

How does one differentiate confidential versus non-confidential information?

The primary thing to look for is whether or not the form contains any identifiable information—something as apparent as an assessment form with a name, or something as innocuous as a payment form with solely a checking account routing number.

What about non-confidential information? Forms such as group or class sign-in sheets, a simple list of names with no detail about each individual, are acceptable. However, a stack of registration forms containing the clients' names plus some information about medical history and previous injuries—what HIPAA refers to as *personal health information*—left on a desk would be a breach. Anything with financial information is strictly confidential.

General respect for a client's privacy is certainly something to take seriously as well. Even though it may not be illegal to have a note with a client's name and weight written on it on your clipboard from a previous session, it is an understood aspect of client-trainer trust that all personal information will be safeguarded. Carelessness is unacceptable.

Fitness professionals must take care to store sensitive information such as registration forms, including health history and financial information, under lock and key. Credit card merchants will end the relationship with any business that fails to properly protect its clients' financial information according to the **merchant agreement**. Additionally, failure to protect this key information results in steep fees.

Good record-keeping is essential to the success of a fitness professional. Not only is it important in understanding the client's history, but it also helps protect the fitness professional and the business or facility, all while maintaining a history of client participation and key events. Let's review several business documents that any fitness professional should know and maintain.

Proper Documentation and Informed Consent

Health fitness professionals should use **informed consent** documents to ensure that clients fully understand the inherent risks of engaging in a training program. These consent forms allow clients to make informed decisions to proceed, while protecting health fitness professionals from liability for injuries that may occur from inherent and treatment risks of the training program.

It is important to note that a **waiver** is still necessary to avoid being liable for injuries that result from negligence. Health fitness professionals should review these documents in detail with their clients, so that an informed decision can be made before both parties agree to move forward. Both the informed consent form and the waiver should comply with state law. Signed consent forms and waivers should be kept on file at all times.

Having a signed waiver prior to an individual's participation in a fitness program is imperative. While a waiver won't protect a group fitness instructor from injuries sustained due to gross neglect on the part of the instructor, it does provide a level of protection in the case of accidents or injuries due to participant error.

It is necessary to work with an attorney while writing the waiver so as to ensure proper coverage. Make sure to consider the types of activities the participant will potentially engage in, as well as any inherent injury risks relative to exercise. State regulations vary, and an attorney will be a key resource in ensuring that the wording of the waiver is appropriate to its specific state's laws.

Key Components for a Liability Waiver should include:
- The name of the health fitness business.
- Any and all potential activities that the training program will include.
- The state where the waiver is being utilized.
- A clear statement regarding the assumption of risk.

Informed Consent

An **informed consent** form communicates to the participant the general nature of what she or he will encounter in the exercise program. It highlights activity type and may emphasize any discomforts that the participant may experience (such as muscle soreness and stiffness). If the instructor will potentially be working physically with the client—taking a physical assessment, for example, or assisting in stretching when touching the client is necessary—then those types of actions may also be outlined. By signing the document, a client is consenting to these actions.

Key Components for an Informed Consent Form should include:
- The name of the health fitness business.
- Clearly list program objectives, benefits, and risks.
- Specify whether or not a physician's consent is required to start the training program or if it is clients' responsibility to do so on their own.

SOAP Note

An excellent tool for documentation is the **SOAP note**. Historically used in the medical field, the SOAP note provides a template for recording information obtained from the client's medical history, and all other information gained throughout their hospitalization. The template applies to the fitness world as well; it is an excellent way of keeping clients' backgrounds and progress organized.

Materials are organized according to subject according to the following:

- **Subjective**: The client's history of exercise, concerns about current health status, or level of fitness, and wellness goals.

- **Objective**: Specific statistics such as weight, girth measurements, body fat percentage, body mass index, and results from a physical assessment.

- **Assessment**: The fitness professional's general findings based on subjective and objective data. Examples are obesity, lack of range of motion in right shoulder due to previous surgery, overly tight hamstrings, etc.

- **Plan**: The plan for the client including recommendations for how to meet their fitness goals.

SOAP notes can then be updated consistently and serve as a running record of the client's progress.

Accidents and injuries in the fitness facility are events any fitness professional hopes to avoid, and proactively working to prevent such issues should always be a priority. Unfortunately, accidents do happen, and it is imperative to have a documentation procedure in place. This established process will ensure consistency among all professionals working at a facility and will help eliminate the proverbial ball being dropped in documentation.

Incident reports, when filled out correctly, provide first-hand, objective information about what happened, and should be completed immediately after the incident. The form typically will include information such as

- Date and location of event.

- Persons involved.

- Witnesses.

- First-hand account of what happened.

- What action was taken and by whom (first aid, CPR, etc.).

- Whether or not an injury was sustained.

- Whether or not medical professionals were contacted.

- Whether or not the injured party refused medical attention.

Signatures of the victim and those facility employee(s) present should also be obtained.

Avoiding incidents that necessitate an incident report form is always best, so employ some basic injury prevention procedures: make sure flooring is even or well-marked at elevation changes; keep equipment in its place; maintain clear walkways; immediately clean up spills; and keep equipment in good condition. These steps will go a long way in preventing accidents and injuries.

RESPONSIBILITIES

As a fitness professional, it is important to understand not only the responsibilities of your profession, but also the limitations of your practice. **Scope of Practice** refers to the range and limits of the responsibilities normally associated with a specific job or function. Issues with Scope of Practice generally arise when first initiating a fitness program: for example, when a client is filling out health-history assessment forms, you will be using said form to determine the client's individual level of fitness. You will never be diagnosing or recommending treatment for a condition. You may need to:

- Refer a participant to a more qualified health professional when necessary.
- Educate a participant about the USDA Dietary Guidelines.
- Recommend and design an exercise program for an average, healthy adult.

ACE outlines the following limitations to the ACE Fitness Professional's Scope of Practice:

1. ACE fitness professionals may NOT "diagnose."

2. ACE fitness professionals may NOT "prescribe."

3. ACE fitness professionals may NOT prescribe diets or recommend specific supplements.

4. ACE fitness professionals may NOT "treat" injury or disease.

5. ACE fitness professionals may NOT "monitor" progress for medically referred clients.

6. ACE fitness professionals may NOT "rehabilitate."

7. ACE fitness professionals may NOT "counsel."

8. ACE fitness professionals may NOT work with "patients."

Health fitness professionals are responsible for client safety, and while prevention should be practiced, you must also be prepared to respond appropriately should an emergency arise. Health fitness professionals who work in health clubs should familiarize themselves with their company's emergency procedures, while independent health fitness professionals should develop their own written plans of action.

Controlling an Emergency Situation

In the case of controlling emergency situations, the best offense is a good defense. Have a plan in mind to prevent emergencies from happening in the first place, and have a backup plan prepared in case those emergencies occur anyway.

Prevention
Health fitness professionals should provide adequate instruction and supervision when working with clients.

For example, a client who is using the treadmill for the first time should be instructed to stand on the runners of the treadmill (straddling the belt) and to hold onto the hand rails before activating the treadmill. This will prevent the client from being taken off guard and being injured when the belt starts to move.

Health fitness professionals must also ensure that all equipment in their facility is regularly inspected, well maintained, and safe for usage. Faulty equipment is an injury waiting to happen.

During an exercise session, pay close attention to each of your clients and keep an eye out for any complications. Stop the exercise session immediately if a client can no longer speak or experiences any of the following: pain, discomfort, nausea, dizziness, lightheadedness, chest pain, an irregular heartbeat, shortness of breath, and/or unusual fatigue.

Emergency Preparedness
A well-prepared health fitness professional reviews his or her clients' medical profiles to ensure as much knowledge about clients as possible.

For example, if a client is diabetic and indicates this on the medical history form, the health fitness professional should then follow up with appropriate questions, potentially request a doctor's consent, and design workouts accordingly, monitoring the client at all times.

Health fitness professionals should also know the steps necessary in a medical emergency.

For example, should a diabetic emergency occur the health fitness professional should call 911, provide adequate care for any life-threatening situations, and give juice or candy to the client or have them take their glucose pill until help arrives.

To further prepare for emergency situations, make sure that you know the appropriate laws for exercise and emergency medical aid within your state and that you maintain the necessary level of insurance as required by your state. Research current industry trends for emergency treatments, and keep your CPR, AED, and Basic Life Support certifications up-to-date.

Clients should have current and accurate PAR-Q forms and medical records on-file, as well as emergency contact numbers. Have the following items nearby and easily accessible: phone numbers for emergency responders and emergency medical devices (CPR micro-shield, first aid kit, AED, etc.). Always plan to follow-up after an emergency within a reasonable time frame.

General Emergency Response Guidelines
Despite your planning and preventative measures, emergencies can always arise. When they do, your preparedness can make all the difference in a critical situation. Knowing how to respond in an emergency can save a person's life, and the faster one responds, the better. Practice can be very helpful to ensure that an emergency is handled calmly and effectively. The following pages detail general guidelines for responding to emergency situations.

Responding to a Seizure
1. Call 911.

2. Lower the person to the ground, on the side if possible.

3. Protect the head from injury by placing a cushion underneath or gently holding it.

4. Turn the person's head to the side.

5. If possible, cover the person's body with a blanket to preserve dignity (some people may lose control of their bowels and/or bladder when seizing).

6. When seizure has ended, place the person in recovery position.

7. Check breathing and pulse.

8. Address any injuries.

9. Comfort the person.

Responding to Shock

1. Monitor the person's breathing and pulse.

2. Keep the person warm.

3. Address any external bleeding.

4. Elevate the legs about twelve inches to maintain circulation. *Avoid doing so if the person is nauseated or having difficulty breathing, may have a neck, head or back injury or potential broken bones, or if moving the person will cause more pain.*

5. Avoid giving the person anything to drink.

Responding to External Bleeding

1. Apply pressure.

2. Apply a bandage.

3. Call 911.

4. Monitor the person's breathing and pulse.

Responding to Choking

1. Call 911.

2. Support the person and lean the body forward.

3. Render five back blows with the heel of your hand.

4. Administer the Heimlich Maneuver. Make a fist and grab it with the other hand. Put the thumb side of your fist against the person's stomach, just above the navel. Administer five thrusts to the abdomen.

5. Continue until the object is forced out or the person is able to breathe or cough on their own.

Responding to Diabetic Emergency

1. Address any life-threatening emergencies.

2. If the person is conscious, give the person fruit juice, non-diet soda, or candy.

3. If the person is conscious, but does not feel better approximately five minutes after taking sugar, call 911 immediately.

4. If the person is unconscious, call 911 immediately.

Musculoskeletal Injuries

Muscle strains, sprains, fractures, joint dislocations and general muscle pain are common injuries that often vary in severity. Administering at-home treatment at the onset of such injuries is fairly simple and usually effective depending on the injury's severity.

It is important to note that if severe trauma is suffered, medical attention should be sought immediately.

In the case of early injury treatment, remember the acronym **R.I.C.E. (Rest, Ice, Compression, and Elevation)**:

Rest: Reduce or stop using the injured area for forty-eight hours. Leg injuries, may require complete rest.

Ice: Apply ice to the injured area for twenty minutes at a time, four to eight times per day. A cold pack, ice bag, or a plastic bag filled with crushed ice can be used.

Compression: Compression may help to reduce swelling. Seek medical advice to determine the best option, but those most commonly used are bandages such as elastic wraps, special boots, air casts, and splints.

Elevation: Elevate the injured area above the level of the heart. Pillows, for example, can be used to help elevate an injured limb.

CREATING SAFE ENVIRONMENTS

The Americans with Disabilities Act

Health fitness professionals who own their own fitness studios are required by the ADA to improve accessibility to those with disabilities. While the ADA does not force small businesses to take on excessive expenses that could be detrimental to the business, small businesses that serve the public must remove physical "barriers" that are "readily achievable," based on their size and the economic means of the business.

For example, small businesses that offer public parking must also provide designated accessible parking spaces that are closest to the entrance. Most entrances to businesses use thirty-six-inch-wide doors that are wide enough to be accessible.

A review of training areas, lounges, locker rooms, restrooms, showers, and counter space should be done to ensure reasonable access for all. Facilities should make every effort to welcome and accommodate those with disabilities.

How to Create a Safe Environment in the Facility You Work In

Maintaining a safe environment for clients is imperative. A great deal of injuries and accidents occur from improper use of equipment and lack of supervision. Promoting safe practices, providing safe equipment, and supervising activity are all good measures towards creating a safe fitness facility.

Tips for creating a safe fitness facility:

- Maintain a clean facility, and encourage workers and clients to do the same by keeping cleaning wipes and/or sanitizer in plain view.

- Only trained professionals should assemble and test exercise equipment prior to use.

- Allow at least 100 square feet of training space for each individual using an area at any given time.

- Inspect and clean equipment regularly; remove any damaged equipment promptly.

- Utilize visuals to describe appropriate usage of equipment.

- Ensure that everyone employed by the facility has current fitness certifications and current CPR certifications.

- Never allow clients to utilize the facility without supervision.

- Encourage clients to bring a small hand towel when working out.

Maintaining Certification

All ACE-certified trainers must maintain certification in CPR and use of an AED. As such, it is within the trainer's scope of practice to utilize these skills in case of emergency until professional medical personnel arrive at the scene. Furthermore, basic first aid may also be applied by a trainer as needed with the consent of the injured person.

Besides maintaining CPR and AED certification, and knowledge of first aid application, an individual must qualify for ACE recertification in other ways.

A trainer must have the ability to communicate and apply appropriate knowledge and skills obtained through completing a total of 2.0 continuing education credits every two years.

Areas of expected knowledge and expertise outside of the construction of a safe and effective group fitness class include:

- Staying abreast of and being able to critically evaluate products and services that are new to the market.

- Having the ability to recognize credible resources, which align with ACE's standards and guidelines.

PROVIDING EDUCATION

Identifying and Accessing Credible Resources

It is recommended that instructors do extensive research before using, endorsing, or recommending alternative methods, products, or services. In extreme cases, legal liability could result if the product, service, or method turns out to be unsafe or harmful. Use the internet with caution.

The United States Department of Agriculture (USDA) and Centers for Disease Control (CDC) also publish good, science-based information and can be contacted with inquiries. As a fitness professional, it is your job to stay up-to-date on the latest research and innovations through continuing education courses, training, and seminars. Be active in the fitness community and establish a network of resources in order to provide reliable sources of data on a host of subjects.

Credible Educational Resources

Joining and keeping up with reputable organizations like the American College of Sports Medicine (ACSM), the American Council on Exercise (ACE), the Aerobics and Fitness Association of America (AFAA), the National Academy of Sports Medicine (NASM), and IDEA Health and Fitness Organization can help instructors and trainers stay educated and informed.

Hypothetical: *A participant comes to you asking for advice on how to make healthful food and beverage selections. What advice could you provide based on food guidelines, labels, and methods of preparation?*

If an instructor or trainer has a nutrition certification, he or she may feel comfortable offering in-depth advice and guidelines. Otherwise, it is advisable to refer clients to reputable websites like www.health.org for help with reading food labels. An instructor may also share personal experiences with nutrition; however, participants should generally be referred to an expert in the field.

Hypothetical: *A participant wants to know about the continued benefits of safe practices and consistent training. What will you tell her?*

An instructor should elaborate on the latest research that highlights the benefits of exercise. It would be appropriate to suggest research found from the reputable sources listed above like the American Council on Exercise (ACE) and the Aerobics and Fitness Association of America (AFAA).

Educational Techniques for Disseminating Information

Clients and participants often have questions and want additional information on fitness topics. Although instructors do their best, it is not always feasible to answer every question in detail. Instructors can educate participants by posting educational information in a central location in the aerobics studio or club. Starting an Internet based newsletter, blog, or Facebook page are also good ways to disseminate information. It is also a good idea to host seminars, facilitated by industry experts, on popular topics.

Final Thoughts

In the end, we know that you will be successful in earning your ACE certification. Although the process can be challenging, if you continue with hard work and dedication, you will find that your efforts will pay off.

If you are struggling after reading this book and following our guidelines, we sincerely hope that you will take note of our advice and seek additional sources for help.

Start by asking friends about the resources that they are using. If you are still not reaching the score you want, consider getting the help of a tutor.

We wish you the best of luck and happy studying!

Most importantly, we admire your drive to enter into the health field—you are putting a lot of work into getting there. Your efforts are sure to pay off.

Sincerely,
The Trivium Test Prep Team

Practice Test

1. Explain a graded exercise test.

2. What form must be obtained by the patient/client prior to a test?

3. Identify three types of metabolic diseases.

4. Give three examples of signs and/or symptoms in individuals with a metabolic disease.

5. Describe the signs and symptoms prompted by exercise in individuals with a neuromuscular disease.

6. What is an appropriate exercise testing method for an individual with a neuromuscular disease?

7. List two absolute contraindications to an exercise test.

8. List four relative contraindications to an exercise test.

9. How is maximal oxygen uptake measured?

10. Which of the following is synonymous with self-efficacy?
    a) Self-Reevaluation.
    b) Self Confidence.
    c) Self-Liberation.
    d) Self-Control.

11. Why are intrinsic rewards more important than extrinsic rewards?
    a) They provide instant motivation for novice fitness participants.
    b) They provide negative feedback to promote correction.
    c) They are internal rewards that ensure permanent adherence to fitness participation.
    d) They eliminate initial barriers to change.

12. In which of the stages of change is it imperative for personal trainers to be the most proactive?
    a) Contemplation.
    b) Preparation.
    c) Action.
    d) Maintenance.

13. If a person vows to quit smoking on their thirtieth birthday, which stage of change are they in?
    a) Pre-Contemplation.
    b) Preparation.
    c) Action.
    d) Maintenance.

14. True or False? Getting a free t-shirt with a paid gym membership is an example of an extrinsic reward.

15. In which of the three learning phases would people rely completely on muscle memory to perform an activity?
   a) Cognitive.
   b) Associative.
   c) Automatic.
   d) None of the above.

16. Which of the following is not an example of active listening?
   a) Using open body language.
   b) Forming a response while someone is speaking.
   c) Allowing a pause after a speaker is finished.
   d) Paraphrasing what a speaker has said.

17. True or False? Behaviorism takes into account an individual's past experiences.

18. People may be in denial about the need for behavior modification during the _____ stage of change in the Trans-theoretical Model.

19. Which of the following is an example of a perceived threat according to the Health Belief Model?
   a) I can't afford a gym membership.
   b) I don't have time to exercise.
   c) I already have pain in my knees.
   d) Fitness machines are boring.

20. True or False? People sometimes fluctuate between the Action and Maintenance stages of change.

21. A patient has auscultating lung sounds, similar to a crackle. What could this mean?

22. True or False? People sometimes fluctuate between the Action and Maintenance stages of change.

23. True or False? Observational learning involves mimicking behavior that appears to be rewarding.

24. True or False? The pros outweigh the cons during the final stages of change in the Trans-theoretical Model of Change.

25. Using a workout video when your friend can't meet you at the gym is an example of:
   a) Counterconditioning.
   b) Self re-evaluation.
   c) Stimulus control.
   d) Decisional Balance.

26. What is another name for the bicuspid valve?

27. Trace the route of blood through the heart.

28. This movement increases the joint's angle and occurs in the sagittal plane around a mediolateral axis.
   a) Rotation.
   b) Flexion.
   c) Circumduction.
   d) Extension.

29. Which of the following is considered a saddle joint?
   a) Hip.
   b) Thumb.
   c) Elbow.
   d) Wrist.

30. Where does gas exchange take place inside the lungs?
   a) Bronchioles.
   b) Pharynx.
   c) Trachea.
   d) Alveoli.

31. Which bioenergetic pathway is sometimes called the "aerobic" pathway?
   a) Oxidative.
   b) Nonoxidative.
   c) Anaerobic.
   d) Phosphagen.

32. What explains how the muscles contract, relax, and/or produce force?
   a) Myosin.
   b) Sliding filament theory.
   c) Sarcomeres.
   d) Actin.

33. Which large protein, usually called the thick filament, is involved with muscle contraction?
   a) Actin.
   b) Sarcomere.
   c) Myosin.
   d) Nuclei.

34. During short duration and high intensity exercises, such as sprinting, which type of muscle fibers are primarily recruited?
   a) Type IIB.
   b) Type I.
   c) Type IIA.
   d) Type III.

35. What is the difference between type I and type II muscle fibers?

36. What is another name for the windpipe?
   a) Larynx.
   b) Trachea.
   c) Pharynx.
   d) Bronchioles.

37. What is the respiratory muscle that allows the human body to breathe?
   a) Femoris.
   b) Triceps.
   c) Diaphragm.
   d) Pectoralis.

38. What term refers to the volume of blood that is ejected out of every ventricle per contraction?
   a) Cardiac Output.
   b) Stroke Volume.
   c) Heart Rate.
   d) End-systolic volume.

39. What is the term used to describe the amount of blood ejected every minute from the left ventricle?
   a) Heart rate.
   b) Stroke volume.
   c) Ejection Fraction.
   d) Cardiac Output.

40. What is the term used when blood is being pulled away from all the vital (visceral) organs of the body to the exercising muscles?
   a) Vasodilation.
   b) Shunting.
   c) Vasoconstriction.
   d) Systole.

41. Which of the following is a beneficial cardiac adaption from long-term cardiovascular exercise?
   a) It decreases resting heart rate.
   b) It results in a slight decrease in resting blood pressure.
   c) It increases stroke volume.
   d) All of the above.

42. What curvature causes a hunching of the back due to excessive outward curving of the spinal column?
   a) Kyphosis.
   b) Scoliosis.
   c) Lordosis.
   d) Hyperlordosis.

43. When elbow flexion is taking place, the bicep will contract while the triceps relax. Which prime mover is the agonist?

44. What tissue holds bones together?
   a) Tendon.
   b) Joint capsule.
   c) Articular cartilage.
   d) Ligament.

45. Name four physiological considerations when designing exercise prescriptions for children.

46. What is a benefit of exercise in older age groups (65 and older)?
   a) Improved psychological and cognitive well-being.
   b) An increase in chronic disease states.
   c) Reduction in physical injuries/impairments.
   d) Both a) and c).
   e) All of the above.

47. Which type of exercise would improve coordination?
   a) Jump rope.
   b) Football.
   c) Swimming.
   d) Yoga.

48. Which factors can affect reaction time?
   a) Age, weight, and coordination.
   b) Practice, experience, strength, and coordination.
   c) Power, agility, and quickness.
   d) All of the above.

49. Intervertebral disks are composed of _____ tissue.
   a) Epithelial.
   b) Fibrocartilaginous.
   c) Muscle.
   d) Heart.

50. Which activities can improve balance?
   a) Running.
   b) Golfing.
   c) Walking.
   d) Gymnastics.

51. Which variables of exercise-program design are recommended to create a progressive training overload?
   a) Frequency.
   b) Equipment.
   c) Difficulty.
   d) Intensity.

52. Which of the following ought to have a designated twenty square-foot area for ideal utilization?
    a) Stability balls.
    b) Tanabatas.
    c) Free Weights.
    d) Medicine balls.

53. How long should a warm-up last?

54. What are the three most common types of eating disorders?

55. What is the most abundant compound of the human body besides fat?

56. How can two people that weigh the same and are the same height look different? Why?

57. Define Waist-to-Hip Ratio.

58. Who should have a higher "normal" body fat percentage – men or women? Why?

59. Name and define the three major types of macronutrients

60. What is a vitamin?

61. What are two common ways to measure body fat?

62. Name four physiological considerations when designing exercise prescriptions for children.

63. What is a benefit of exercise in older age groups (65 and older)?
    a) Improved psychological and cognitive well-being.
    b) An increase in chronic disease states.
    c) Reduction in physical injuries/impairments.
    d) Both a) and c).
    e) All of the above.

64. What type of test measures how well the lungs are oxygenating blood in patients being assessed for COPD?
    a) Chest X-ray.
    b) Pulmonary Function Test.
    c) Arterial Blood Gas Analysis.
    d) CT scan.

65. Which of the following is a non-modifiable risk factor for CVD?
    a) Smoking.
    b) Gender.
    c) Hypertension.
    d) Dyslipidemia.
    e) Type II Diabetes.

66. Which medication is used in the treatment of mild hypertension?
   a) Calcium Channel Blockers.
   b) Nitrates.
   c) Beta Blockers.
   d) Diuretics.

67. List five signs and symptoms of Cardiopulmonary Disease.

68. The effects of exercise on coronary artery disease risk factors are:
   a) A decrease in resting and exercise blood pressure.
   b) A decrease in total cholesterol, LDL cholesterol, and triglycerides.
   c) An increase in HDL cholesterol.
   d) Improved glucose tolerance and insulin sensitivity.
   e) All of the above.

69. List four characteristics of transmural ischemia with myocardial infarction.

70. The following are steps to assist in behavior adherence:
   a) Assess the individual's medical needs.
   b) Identify specific medication goals.
   c) Plan the teaching-learning and behavioral change process.
   d) Establish support.
   e) All of the above

71. Name 3 types (classes) of antianginals.

72. Which is an example of an antianginal medication?
   a) Toprol.
   b) Nitroquick.
   c) Lasix.
   d) Both a) and b).
   e) None of the above.

73. Which is a side effect of diuretics?
   a) Tachycardia.
   b) Headaches.
   c) Postural Hypotension.
   d) Blurred vision.

74. List three characteristics of amiodarone.

75. What are the three types of insulin used in diabetes management?

76. Which of the following is/are side effect(s) of Tricyclic antidepressants (TCAs)?
   a) Bradycardia.
   b) Hypertension.
   c) Left and/or Right Bundle Branch Blocks on ECG.
   d) Both b) and c).
   e) All of the above.

77. Name five kinds of anti-platelet medications.

78. List four reasons why alcohol consumption and exercise are contraindicated.

79. The following is an excellent educational source for fitness professionals:
   a) The NRA.
   b) The BBC.
   c) ACE.
   d) NBC.

80. How can an aerobics instructor enhance his or her skill set and knowledge of health and fitness?
   a) Attend fitness industry conferences.
   b) Go back to school.
   c) Take new classes.
   d) Pursue national certifications.

81. How is a radial pulse check done?

82. Which of the following are not serious signs of dehydration?
   a) Chest pain.
   b) Confusion.
   c) Vomiting.
   d) Coughing.

83. Factors that can affect a person's training heart rate are:
   a) Medications.
   b) Caffeine.
   c) Altitude.
   d) Too much water.

84. What is the formula for calculating one's training zone?

85. Which of the following is NOT a benefit of an exercise program?
   a) Decreased body fat.
   b) Decreased blood pressure.
   c) Increased risk of Type II Diabetes.
   d) Increased metabolism.

86. Explain the difference between moderate intensity exercise and vigorous intensity exercise.

87. The level of demand that an activity places on the body is:
   a) Resistance.
   b) Weight.
   c) Intensity
   d) Frequency.

88. The ACSM suggests what amount of time of continuous physical activity for general health requirements?

89. Determine the target heart rate zone of a thirty-year-old client with a resting heart rate of sixty-five bpm.

90. _____ represents an individual's resting metabolism or oxygen uptake, and is a way for you to measure the intensity of your workouts.

91. What should your focus be during the first six months of training and conditioning?

92. When muscles are contracting concentrically an individual should
   a) inhale.
   b) exhale.
   c) hold his or her breath.
   d) None of the above.

93. A lengthening of the muscle fibers is what type of action?
   a) Isometric.
   b) Concentric.
   c) Flexibility.
   d) Eccentric.

94. Define the progression principle.

95. How often should children between ages five and twelve participate in exercise?
   a) Once a week.
   b) Every other day, for three hours at a time.
   c) Every day, for sixty minutes.
   d) Only when they request exercise.

96. List the five essential exercise components affecting the attainment of physical fitness.

97. Which of the following is not an aerobic exercise?
   a) Cross-country skiing.
   b) Swimming.
   c) Strength training.
   d) Walking.

98. True or False? Chronic adaptions occur during an exercise session.

99. Which of the following is not a chronic disease?
   a) Cardiovascular disease.
   b) Pulmonary disease.
   c) Diabetes.
   d) Obesity.

100. True or False? Chronic diseases are diseases of long duration and are generally slow in progression.

101. True or False? Many people with Type II Diabetes are relatively inactive and overweight, or obese.

102. True or False? Exercise testing elicits the body's reaction to measured increases in acute exercise.

103. True or False? Aerobic exercise is usually short in duration, but high in intensity.

104. Which of the following is not defined as a resistance exercise?
   a) Lunges.
   b) Push-ups.
   c) Swimming.
   d) Bench press.

105. True or False? Exercising at a high altitude affects breathing rate, which increases the amount of oxygen into and out of the lungs.

106. Which of the following is not an absolute indication in exercise testing?
   a) Suspicion of a myocardial infarction or acute myocardial infarction (heart attack).
   b) Severe or unusual shortness of breath.
   c) Any chest pain that is increasing.
   d) Severe or unusual shortness of breath.

107. True or False? Hyperglycemia can be defined as low blood sugar.

108. True or False? Blurred vision is a symptom of hyperglycemia.

109. True or False? If a client shows symptoms of Hypoglycemia, he or she can resume activity once the blood glucose level reaches 100 mg/dL.

110. True or False? It is normal for a person's heart to pump at 100 beats per minute or faster.

111. True or False? It is probably safe for clients with diabetes to work out at high altitudes.

112. True or False? A person with tachycardia may never show symptoms.

113 True or False? Strenuous exercise can cause sudden death in non-athletes.

114. True or False? Type I diabetes occurs when the body is insulin resistant.

115. True or False? Proper instruction and supervision can help prevent injuries.

116. The appropriate response to a diabetic emergency is to:
    a) Call 911 if the person is unconscious.
    b) Give the person fruit juice.
    c) Address any life threatening injuries.
    d) All of the above.

117. True or False? A trainer cannot be sued for negligence if the client signed a consent form.

118. Emergency preparedness includes taking the following steps:
    a) Purchase a fire extinguisher.
    b) Maintain current CPR, AED, and Basic Life Support certifications.
    c) Make sure the client drinks water during the workout.
    d) Have the client sign a waiver.

119. If a client has a seizure, the trainer should:
    a) Lay them on their back.
    b) Go outside and wait for the ambulance.
    c) Restrain the client.
    d) Protect the client's head from injury and place a cushion underneath it.
    e) All of the above.

120. An exercise session should be stopped immediately:
    a) If the client thinks it is too hard.
    b) If the client experiences chest pain.
    c) To make a phone call.
    d) To check the client's pulse.
    e) None of the above.

121. True or False? If a client goes into shock, give the client something to drink.

122. A waiver should include the following info:
    a) The client's date of birth.
    b) The name of the personal training business or club.
    c) The client's workout goals.
    d) The trainer's phone number.

123. True or False? Elevating a person's legs when they go into shock helps to keep the blood circulating.

124. During a diabetic emergency:
    a) Perform CPR.
    b) Keep the person warm.
    c) Call 911 before doing anything else.
    d) None of the above.

125.   Musculoskeletal injuries include:
a)   Joint dislocations.
b)   Bruises.
c)   Nose bleeds.
d)   Headaches.

126.   How much space should be maintained between exercise equipment in a fitness facility?
a)   A few inches.
b)   200 feet.
c)   Fifty feet.
d)   100 feet.

127.   True or False? An absolute contraindication to exercise means it is okay to work out under a doctor's supervision.

128.   R.I.C.E (rest, ice, compression and elevate) is best administered:
a)   Forty-eight hours after the injury occurred.
b)   In the morning.
c)   At the onset of the injury.
d)   When there is bruising.

129.   True or False? The cool down should produce the opposite effect of the warm up when done properly.

130.   ADA guidelines include which of the following:
a)   Doors should be thirty-six inches wide.
b)   If public parking is provided, designated disabled spaces should also be provided.
c)   Adequate space for wheelchairs to maneuver inside the facility.
d)   All of the above.

131.   Define the purpose of the cool down.
a)   To get the body ready for exercise.
b)   To mimic exercises done during the workout.
c)   To transition the body from activity back to a resting state.
d)   None of the above.

132.   Which is an example of accident prevention?
a)   Removing faulty or broken equipment.
b)   Encouraging clients to warm up and cool down.
c)   Providing towels to clients free of charge.
d)   Keep an AED in the fitness facility.

133.   True or False? A warm-up should be two or three minutes in duration.

134. Which is an example of a relative contraindication to exercise testing?
    a) Mental impairment leading to an inability to cooperate.
    b) Severe hypertension.
    c) Inability to speak English.
    d) Being deaf.

135. True or False? Clients with osteoporosis should avoid weight training altogether.

136. The three type of stretches are: (circle all that apply)
    a) Passive.
    b) Aggressive.
    c) Active.
    d) Ballistic.

137. Stretches should be held for a minimum of:
    a) Thirty seconds.
    b) One minute.
    c) Two minutes.
    d) As long as you want.

138. Which is a short-term effect of exercise?
    a) Weight loss.
    b) Mobility.
    c) Increased metabolism.
    d) All of the above.

139. An example of failure to comply with ACE's Professional Practices includes which of the following?
    a) Unauthorized possession, use, access, or distribution of certification examinations, score reports, trademarks, logos, written materials, answer sheets, certificates, certificate holder or applicant files, or other confidential or proprietary ACE documents or materials (registered or otherwise).

    b) Any temporary or permanent physical, mental, or emotional condition, including, but not limited to, substance abuse, which could impair competent and objective professional performance.

    c) Negligent and/or intentional misconduct in professional work.

    d) All of the above.

140. The guidelines for storing credit card information are specified in:
    a) The facility/gym's policies.
    b) The instructor or personal trainer's contract.
    c) The client's request.
    d) The credit card merchant agreement.

141. What document provides a layer of protection in the case of accidents or injuries due to participant error?
    a) Informed consent.
    b) Waiver.
    c) Professional liability insurance certificate.
    d) Sign-in sheet.

142. Which section of the SOAP note is where one would note the fitness professional's general findings based on subjective and objective data?
    a) Subjective.
    b) Objective.
    c) Assessment.
    d) Plan.

143. Which of the following are examples of the type of information that should be included when completing an incident report?
    a) What action was taken and by whom.
    b) The instructor's opinion of who was at fault.
    c) Whether or not medical professionals were contacted.
    d) Both a) and c).

144. Which is NOT a limitation of the ACE trainer's scope of practice?
    a) Diagnose.
    b) Design an exercise program.
    c) Prescribe diets or recommend specific supplements.
    d) Treat injury or disease.

145. A key component to minimizing risk is
    a) Incorporating an adequate warm-up and cool-down.
    b) Getting enough sleep prior to teaching a class.
    c) Choosing music the participants like.
    d) Creating innovative choreography to create excitement among participants.

146. Describe a duty.

147. What are the four basic duties of a health fitness professional?

148. Which of the following statements concerning needs assessments is true?
    a) They are no help with the evaluation of a program.
    b) They are useful for marketing purposes.
    c) The needs assessment is a planning process that involves gathering sufficient and appropriate data, which will be directed towards developing and implementing a feasible and applicable solution.
    d) They are used to make management happy.

149. What is a PAR-Q form used for?
   a) It is a legal form.
   b) Budget assessment.
   c) Self-screening tool.
   d) Policies and procedures.

150. True or False? Aerobics instructors, even though they may not hold a nutrition degree or certification, should feel comfortable giving nutrition and dietary advice.

Practice Test: Answers

1. This test measures **functional capacity**. The test will use an estimated VO2 max, unless the spirometer is used to get an actual VO2 max. Also, a test exceeding seven minutes indicates prognostic cardiovascular fitness value, due to the increased work capacity. The most basic and most widely-used exercise test is the Bruce Protocol treadmill test, which increases speed and elevation every three minutes, with the patient walking or running until they are impeded by either exhaustion or a contraindication.

2. **Informed Consent**.

3. Obesity, Diabetes Mellitus I and II, thyroid disease, renal disease, and liver disease.

4. **High blood sugar levels** (sign of diabetes mellitus and obesity); shakiness and disorientation (symptoms of hypoglycemia); weight gain, sluggish behavior, and hair loss (indicative of hypothyroidism).

5. High sensitivity to hot or cold temperatures; lower extremity muscle weakness; foot drop; loss of sensation and/or balance/coordination; and tremors of varying degrees.

6. An appropriate test would be a low-impact machine, such as a cycle ergometer.

7. The following are all correct answers:
   - Acute myocardial infarction.
   - Unstable angina.
   - Uncontrolled cardiac arrhythmias.
   - Symptomatic severe aortic stenosis.
   - Uncontrolled symptomatic heart failure.
   - Acute pulmonary embolus or pulmonary infarction.
   - Acute myocarditis or pericarditis.
   - Acute aortic dissection.
   - Suspected or known dissection aneurysm.
   - Acute system infection, accompanied by fever, body aches, or swollen lymph glands.

8. The following are all correct answers:
   - Left main coronary stenosis.
   - Moderate stenotic valvular heart disease.
   - Electrolyte abnormalities, such as hypokalemia or hypomagnesaemia.
   - Severe arterial hypertension (greater than 200 mmHg and/or diastolic BP greater than 110 mmHg at rest).
   - Tachyarrhythmias or bradyarrhythmias.
   - Hypertrophic cardiomyopathy and/or other forms of outflow tract obstruction.
   - Neuromuscular, musculoskeletal, or rheumatoid disorders that could be exacerbated by exercise.
   - Ventricular aneurysm.

- Uncontrolled metabolic disease, such as diabetes, thyrotoxicosis, or myxedema.
- Chronic infectious diseases such as mononucleosis, hepatitis, or AIDS.
- Mental or physical impairment leading to inability to exercise adequately.
- High-degree atrioventricular block.

9. Maximal oxygen uptake (VO2 max) is a measure of cardiorespiratory fitness. It is a product of maximal cardiac output and arterial–venous oxygen difference. It is measured through an open circuit spirometer.

10. **b)** Self Confidence.

11. **c)** They are internal rewards that ensure permanent adherence to fitness participation.

12. **c)** Action.

13. **b)** Preparation.

14. **True**.

15. **c)** Automatic.

16. **b)** Forming a **response while someone is speaking**.

17. **False**.

18. **Pre-contemplation**.

19. **c)** I already have pain in my knees.

20. **True**.

21. This indicates **fluid in the lungs**.

22. **True**.

23. **True**.

24. **True**.

25. **a)** Counterconditioning.

26. The **Mitral valve** is another name for the bicuspid valve that separates the left atrium from the left ventricle.

27. Review the image.

28. d) Extension.

29. b) Thumb. The saddle joint provides flexion, extension, abduction, adduction, and circumduction.

30. d) Alveoli. Alveoli are tiny air sacs where gases are exchanged between the lungs and blood.

31. a) Oxidative. The oxidative system is also called the aerobic pathway because oxygen is required for this pathway to work.

32. b) Sliding filament theory.

33. c) Myosin.

34. a) Type IIB. Type IIB fibers are fast twitch fibers; these fibers can produce bursts of power, but they fatigue quickly.

35. Type II fibers are for high intensity and short duration exercises (sprinting and weightlifting). **Type I fibers** are for low intensity and long duration exercise (marathon running).

36. b) Trachea.

37. c) Diaphragm.

38. b) Stroke volume.

39. d) Cardiac Output.

40. b) Shunting.

41. d) All of the above.

42. a) Kyphosis. Kyphosis curvature is excessive outwards of the spinal that causes hunching of the back. These are curves in the thoracic and sacral regions.

43. Bicep.

44. d) Ligament.

45. The following are all correct answers:
- Higher maximal and submaximal oxygen uptake.
- Higher resting and exercising heart rates.
- Lower resting and exercising blood pressures.
- Hormonal changes.

- Thermoregulatory differences.
- Muscle and bone formation.
- Body composition.

46. d) Both **a)** and **c)** are benefits.

47. a). Jump rope.

48. b). Practice, experience, strength, and coordination.

49. b) Fibrocartilaginous. Between each vertebra are intervertebral disks. These disks are flat and round and are composed of fibrocartilaginous tissue. This tissue is strong and tough; it allows for slight movement.

50. c). Walking.

51. a) and d). (Frequency and Intensity).

52. c). Free weights.

53. Five to ten minutes.

54. Anorexia Nervosa, Bulimia Nervosa, Binge-Eating Disorder.

55. Water.

56. They have **different body compositions**; i.e., they can weigh the same, but since muscle weighs more than fat, one person could be more fit than another, even if they have the same height and weight.

57. A waist to hip ratio (WHR) is a fraction that represents the **circumference of the waist divided by the circumference of the hip**.

58. Women have a higher percentage of body fat due to **childbearing** characteristics.

59. Carbohydrates: Carbohydrates are the most important source of energy for the body. The digestive system changes carbohydrates into glucose (blood sugar). The body uses this sugar for energy for cells, tissues, and organs.

Proteins: Proteins are made of chains of amino acids and are the building blocks of life. The body needs proteins to repair and maintain essential structures and functions. Every cell in the human body contains protein. It is a major part of the skin, muscles, organs, and glands. Protein is also found in all body fluids, except bile and urine.

Lipids: Lipids are various substances that are not soluble in water and include fats, waxes, phospholipids, cerebrosides, and related or derived compounds.

60. Vitamins are any of a group of organic compounds that are essential for normal growth and nutrition and are required in small quantities in the diet. They are important because they cannot be synthesized by the body and are essential to survival.

61. Skinfold measurements and **bioelectric impedance analysis**.

62. The following are all correct answers:
- Higher maximal and submaximal oxygen uptake.
- Higher resting and exercising heart rates.
- Lower resting and exercising blood pressures.
- Hormonal changes.
- Thermoregulatory differences.
- Muscle and bone formation.
- Body composition.

63. d) Both **a)** and **c)** are benefits.

64. c) Arterial Blood Gas Analysis.

65. b) Gender.

66. d) Diuretics.

67. The following are all correct answers:
- Pain or discomfort in the chest, neck, jaw, or back.
- Resting dyspnea or dizziness.
- Nocturnal dyspnea.
- Orthopnea.
- Ankle edema.
- Palpitations.
- Claudications.
- Heart Murmurs.
- Unusual fatigue.

68. b) All of the above.

69. The following are all correct answers:
- Changes in both QRS and ST complexes.
- ST elevation or Tall, upright T-waves early on.
- Q waves in a few hours after onset.
- ST elevation may return to baseline and T wave invert.
- Q waves may persist for years; T wave inversion may indefinitely.

70. c) Plan the teaching-learning and behavioral change process.

71. Beta Adrenergic Blockers, Nitrates, Calcium Channel Antagonists.

72. d) Both a) and b).

73. c) Postural Hypotension.

74. Used to treat ventricular tachycardia, ventricular fibrillation, and atrial fibrillation; shows beta blocker-like and potassium channel blocker-like actions on the SA and AV node; increases the refractory period via sodium and potassium channel effects which slow intracardiac conduction.

75. Rapid, Intermediate, and Long-acting insulin are all used in Diabetes management.

76. d) Both b) and c).

77. Aspirin, Plavix, Persantine, Aggrenox, Ticlid.

78. Decreased recovery time, increase in body fat percentage, disrupted sleep, and depletion of water and nutrients.

79. c). ACE

80. a), b), c), and **d)**.

81. By using one hand to locate the pulse on the thumb side of the opposite wrist. While holding the hand, palm facing up, the index and middle fingers are used touch the artery and feel the pulse.

82. a) and **d)**. Chest pain and coughing.

83. a), b), and **c)**. Medications, caffeine and altitude.

84. HRR (heart rate reserve) * Intensity % + RHR (resting heart rate).

85. c) Increased risk of Type II Diabetes.

Exercise keeps your heart in good health, decreases body fat, creates lean muscle mass, increases metabolism, reduces risk of osteoporosis, arthritis, type II Diabetes, decreases blood pressure and cholesterol, and boosts self-esteem.

86. Moderate-intensity exercise puts enough demand on the body during aerobic exercise to increase heart rate and respiratory rates. Ex. Walking, climbing the stairs, mowing the yard.

Vigorous-intensity exercise is more intense than moderate intensity exercise and causes an even greater increase in heart rate. Ex. Running, playing an intense sport.

87. **c)** Intensity.

88. Twenty to sixty minutes.

89. Target heart rate = 144-168.

90. METs.

91. You should focus on developing basic strength and endurance, flexibility, efficient connective and supportive systems, stabilization, proper movement patterns, and cardiovascular fitness.

92. **a)** Inhale.

93. **d)** Eccentric.

94. The **progression principle** states that there is a desired level of overload that should be achieved in an optimal amount of time.

95. **c)** Every day, for sixty minutes.

96. **Mode, Frequency, Intensity, Duration,** and **Progression**.

97. **c)** Strength training (the use of resistance for muscular contraction to build the strength, anaerobic endurance, and size of skeletal muscles).

98. **False**. Chronic adaptations occur with long-term aerobic and resistance training. They occur over a period of time and can usually be seen as early as 6 weeks.

99. **d) Obesity**.

100. **True**. Chronic diseases are diseases of long duration, generally slow in progression.

101. **True**. Many people with Type II Diabetes are relatively inactive and overweight or obese, particularly with excessive abdominal fat.

102. **True**. Exercise testing elicits the body's reaction to measured increases in acute exercise.

103. **False**. Aerobic exercise is usually long in duration, but low in intensity.

104. **c) Swimming** (defined as an aerobic exercise).

105. **False**. Exercising at a high altitude affects breathing rate, which can decrease the amount of oxygen into and out of the lungs. An increase in altitude decreases the partial pressure of oxygen and reduces the amount of oxygen bound to hemoglobin (protein in the blood that carries oxygen).

106. **c)** Any increasing chest pain is a **relative indication**.

107. **False**.

108. **True**.

109. **True**.

110. **False**.

111. **False**.

112. **True**.

113. **True**.

114. **False**.

115. **True**.

116. **d)** All of the above.

117. **False**.

118. **b)** Maintain current CPR, AED, and Basic Life Support certifications.

119. **d)** Protect the client's head from injury and place a cushion underneath it.

120. **b)** The client experiences chest pain.

121. **False**.

122. **b)** The name of the personal training business or club.

123. **True**.

124. **d)** None of the above. In a diabetic emergency, first address any life-threatening emergencies. If the person is conscious, provide fruit juice, non-diet soda, or candy. If the person is conscious, but does not feel better approximately five minutes after taking sugar, call 911 immediately. If the person is unconscious, call 911 immediately.

125. **a)** Joint dislocations.

126. **d)** 100 feet.

127. **False**.

128. **c)** At the onset of the injury.

129. **True**.

130. **d)** All of the above.

131. **c)** To transition the body from activity back to a resting state.

132. **a)** Removing faulty or broken equipment.

133. **False**.

134. **a)** Mental impairment leading to an inability to cooperate.

135. **False**.

136. **a)** Passive; **c)** Active; and **d)** Ballistic.

137. **a)** Thirty seconds.

138. **c)** Increased metabolism.

139. **d)** All of the above.

140. **d)** The credit card merchant agreement.

141. **b)** Waiver.

142. **c)** Assessment.

143. **d)** Both **a)** and **c)**What action was taken and by whom; and Whether or not medical professionals were contacted.

144. **b)** Design an exercise program.

145. **a)** Incorporating an adequate warm-up and cool-down.

146. **A duty** is a **legal obligation,** something that someone else is supposed to do under contract.

147. There are four basic duties that they should abide by: **Inform, Instruct, Monitor, and Supervise**.

148. **c) Needs Assessment** is a systematic process for determining and addressing needs that may be needed for the improvement in individuals within a community or organization. The

needs assessment is a planning process that involves gathering sufficient and appropriate data that will be directed towards developing and implementing a feasible and applicable solution.

149. **c)** The physical activity readiness questionnaire **(PAR-Q)** is a self-screening tool that can be used by anyone who is planning to start an exercise program. It is often used by fitness trainers or coaches to determine the safety or possible risk of exercising for an individual based upon their answers to specific health history questions.

150. **False.**

Made in the USA
Middletown, DE
19 December 2017